Twayne's United States Authors Series

Sylvia E. Bowman, *Editor*

INDIANA UNIVERSITY

Kenneth Rexroth

Courtesy of Morgan Gibson

KENNETH REXROTH

By MORGAN GIBSON
Goddard College

 208

Twayne Publishers, Inc. :: New York

FOR MY FATHER AND MOTHER

Preface

After half a century of writing some of the most remarkable poems of love and solitude, prophetic revolt and philosophical contemplation in modern literature, Kenneth Rexroth has emerged, I believe, as one of America's wisest living poets. In his *Collected Shorter Poems* and *Collected Longer Poems,* the dramatic tetralogy *Beyond the Mountains,* eight volumes of translations from Asian and Western languages, six collections of critical essays, and *An Autobiographical Novel,* his life and thought have become universalized in a vision of reality as community. Amazing erudition, deep feeling, and transcendent clarity of perception unite in an integral person communing with nature and with those he loves, both living and dead. He has stood firm against a dehumanizing world of war, bureaucratic repression, runaway technology, and self-alienation. He has been saved from despair by a kind of religious anarchism which he has described variously as "erotic mysticism," "anthropological religion," and "organic philosophy," invoking comparisons with the visionary dimensions of D. H. Lawrence, William Blake, and Walt Whitman. Moreover, Rexroth's radical sense of responsibility for all mankind suffering in the creative process of the universe expresses his personal transmutation of Classical, Christian, and Oriental traditions in the tragic context of modern thought and experience. An original American independent like Henry David Thoreau and Mark Twain, he is as cosmopolitan as Ezra Pound and T. S. Eliot, but he is more rooted in common humanity.

As a philosophical poet concerned primarily with communicating visionary experience, Rexroth has experimented with styles ranging from "the Revolution of the Word" to direct statement in the tradition of Chinese and Japanese poetry and the Greek Anthology, which he has perfected as his most characteristic style. He has won many important awards and grants, and his reputation in Europe and Japan is high. However, his poems seldom appear in American quarterlies and anthologies; and only a few short essays about his work, in addition to reviews of individual books, have been published so far. One reason may be that, as a San Francisco poet, he has carried on an unceasing battle against the New York cultural establishment (though his own publisher, New Directions, is located in New York). The New Critics ignored him, and he lambasted the "southern colonels" and "corn-belt metaphysicals" who were insisting, during the Korean War, that poetic experimentation and social revolt were finished.

However, poets as diverse as William Carlos Williams, Richard Eberhart, John Ciardi, Muriel Rukeyser, Dudley Fitts, and William Stafford, among others, have loved and praised his poetry for years; and he is an honored mentor of the generation of Allen Ginsberg, Denise Levertov, Gary Snyder, Lawrence Ferlinghetti, Michael McClure, and Brother Antoninus, who helped revolutionize American poetry in the 1950's and who continue to "make it new." So does Rexroth, the vitality of his mind permeating each new book of his poetry and prose.

I have written this book to put in order my thoughts concerning the poet who, more than any other, has helped me understand poetry as communion, communication of vision, and communal sacrament. His work has helped liberate my own poetry and sense of tradition—my consciousness of actuality most of all—and I hope that I do justice to his achievement.

"Poetry as Personal Communion," my opening chapter, is a discussion of his visionary esthetics in relation to his personality as revealed in *An Autobiographical Novel* as well as poems. Chapter 2, "Despair and Revolt between World Wars," covers his poetry from 1920 to 1940: *The Homestead Called Damascus, The Art of Worldly Wisdom,* and *In What Hour.* In Chapter 3, I discuss "Love as Universal Responsibility" in *The Phoenix and the Tortoise* and in *The Signature of All Things.* Chapter 4, "Drama and Dialectic of Community," is an analysis of two companion works of the early 1950's: the tragic tetralogy *Beyond the Mountains* and the philosophical epic, *The Dragon and the Unicorn,* based on his European travels. "Polemics and Elegies of the Atomic Age," Chapter 5, covers Rexroth's role in the San Francisco Renaissance, *In Defense of the Earth, Natural Numbers,* translations, and essays. And in Chapter 6, "The Climax of the Rite of Rebirth," I assess his poetic achievement to date by focusing on *The Collected Shorter Poems* and *The Collected Longer Poems.*

Contents

Acknowledgments

First of all, I wish to thank Kenneth Rexroth, who has been extraordinarily patient and helpful in correspondence as well as on many occasions when I have had the opportunity to discuss his work with him: first, during the summer of 1964, when he was writer-in-residence at the University of Wisconsin —Milwaukee; second, during the summer of 1966, when my wife and I visited him in San Francisco; and third, during the spring of 1968, when I accompanied him on a reading tour of Wisconsin and Illinois. His secretaries Carol Tinker and Diane Jarreau also deserve my gratitude.

It is impossible to thank everyone who has contributed to my appreciation of Rexroth's work. I have discussed it with Denise Levertov, Allen Ginsberg, Michael McClure, Brother Antoninus, Paul Goodman, Robert Bly, James Wright, Walter Lowenfels, and others. Professor James Delaplain, formerly of the University of Wisconsin—Milwaukee, offered some initial suggestions; and Brooke Whiting, Literary Manuscripts Librarian at the University of California at Los Angeles, supplied me with the checklist of Rexroth's publications and information about the collection of his papers in the University Library there. Discussion with students in my graduate seminar in modern literature and my creative writing classes at the University of Wisconsin—Milwaukee, as well as in a seminar on anarchism and avant-garde literature in the Free University of Milwaukee, sponsored by Students for a Democratic Society, has thrown additional light on Rexroth's work. I am especially grateful to Barbara Browne Gibson for many insights into Rexroth's work from a feminist point of view. Dalana Lillich, Jef Hinich, and Kathryn Erdman, my student assistants, have helped with the bibliography.

Kenneth Rexroth and the following publishers have kindly granted permission to reprint passages from his books:

New Directions Publishing Corporation: *The Phoenix and the Tortoise*, Copyright 1944 by New Directions Publishing Corporation; D. H. Lawrence, *Selected Poems* (Introduction by

I also wish to thank the Graduate School of the University of Wisconsin—Milwaukee for providing me with travel funds for a trip to San Francisco during the summer of 1966, when I did preliminary research for this book.

MORGAN GIBSON

Goddard College

Chronology

1905   Kenneth Rexroth born on December 22, 1905, in South Bend, Indiana. Ancestors were German scholars, German-American radicals, and American Indians. His parents—Charles Rexroth, a pharmacist, and Delia (or Della) Reed Rexroth—were culturally advanced, maintaining a circle of literary and artistic friends. The family moved to Elkhart, Indiana, a few months after his birth.

1912   After a European tour, the Rexroths lived in Battle Creek, Michigan, where Charles failed in business and Delia contracted tuberculosis.

1915-   Family moved to Chicago and then back to Elkhart, where
1916   mother died of gangrene of the lung.

1916-   Kenneth lived in Toledo, Ohio, with his paternal grand-
1918   mother and then his father, who, after business failures, died of alcoholism.

1918-   Lived with aunt on Chicago's South Side in James T. Far-
1921   rell's neighborhood. Attended Englewood High School and the Art Institute; audited classes at the University of Chicago. Precociously active as painter, poet, actor, director, journalist, and political radical.

1921   Worked his way to the West Coast and back to Chicago.

1922   During a love affair with Leslie Smith ("Shirley Johnson"), a social worker, he wrote *The Homestead Called Damascus,* his first long philosophical reverie (not published until 1957).

1926   Worked his way to Europe on a ship and back, then across the United States to the Far West, Mexico, and back to Chicago.

1927   Married Andrée Dutcher; moved to San Francisco. Finished his second long poem, "Prolegomena to a Theodicy" (published as "A Prolegomenon to a Theodicy" in *The Art of Worldly Wisdom,* 1949).

1940   Politically active on the Left during the Depression. Andrée died. *In What Hour,* his first book (for which he received the California Literature Silver Medal Award in 1941). Married Marie Kass, a nurse.

1944   *The Phoenix and the Tortoise,* his second book (for which he received another California Literature Silver Medal Award in 1945).

1948 Divorced from Marie. Traveled in Europe on a Guggenheim Fellowship, renewed in 1949.

1949 *The Art of Worldly Wisdom,* his third book, containing early poems, 1920-30, published, as well as his anthology, *The New British Poets.* Married Marthe Larsen.

1950 Birth of daughter Mary. *The Signature of All Things,* his fourth book of poems.

1951 *Beyond the Mountains,* four plays modeled on Greek tragedy and Japanese Nōh, published as a book.

1952 *The Dragon and the Unicorn,* a long philosophical travel poem, published as his fifth book of poetry.

1954 Birth of daughter Katherine.

1955 *A Bestiary for My Daughters Mary and Katherine* and *Thou Shalt Not Kill: A Memorial for Dylan Thomas*—his sixth and seventh books of original poetry—published, as well as translations: *One Hundred Poems from the Japanese* and *One Hundred French Poems.*

1956 Led the San Francisco Renaissance; announced the Beat Generation, which he later criticized. Taught at San Francisco State College. *In Defense of the Earth,* containing the *Bestiary* and *Thou Shalt Not Kill,* published as his eighth book of original poetry, and translations: *One Hundred Poems from the Chinese* and *Thirty Spanish Poems of Love and Exile.*

1957 Received a Chapelbrook Award and the Eunice Teitjens Award from *Poetry* magazine.

1958 *The Homestead Called Damascus,* the long poem completed in 1925, published in *The Quarterly Review of Literature* (and in 1963 republished as his ninth book of original poetry): for it, he received a Longview Award. Also received the $1,000 Shelley Memorial Award from the Poetry Society of America and an Amy Lowell Fellowship.

1959 *Bird in the Bush: Obvious Essays.*

1961 Divorced from Marthe. His second book of criticism, *Assays.*

1962 *Poems from the Greek Anthology.*

1963 *Natural Numbers: New and Selected Poems* (his tenth book of original poetry).

1964 Grant from the National Academy of Arts and Letters. Taught at San Francisco State College and, in the summer, at the University of Wisconsin—Milwaukee.

1965 William Carlos Williams Award from *Contact* magazine.

1966 *The Collected Shorter Poems* (his eleventh book of poetry) and *An Autobiographical Novel.*

1967 Traveled around the world on a grant from the Rockefeller Foundation and an Akademische Austauschdienst Award from

Chronology

West Germany. *The Heart's Garden / The Garden's Heart* (his twelfth book of original poetry).

1968   *The Collected Longer Poems* (his thirteenth book of original poetry) and *Classics Revisited,* essays collected from *Saturday Review* (his third book of criticism). Teaching at the University of California at Santa Barbara.

1969   Translations of Pierre Reverdy.

1970   More Chinese translations: *Love in the Turning Year.* His fourth and fifth books of criticism: *With Eye and Ear* and *The Alternative Society: Essays from the Other World.*

1971   *American Poetry in the Twentieth Century* (his sixth book of criticism) and *Sky Sea Birds Trees Earth House Beasts Flowers* (poetry) published.

CHAPTER 1

Poetry as Personal Communion

I *"A Letter to William Carlos Williams"*

KENNETH REXROTH embodies William Wordsworth's idea of a poet as "a man speaking to men—a man, it is true, endowed with more lively sensibility, more enthusiasm and tenderness, who has greater knowledge of human nature, and a more comprehensive soul, than are supposed to be common among mankind."[1] Most of Rexroth's poetry is direct personal communication addressed to his family, friends, lovers, poets, or readers as confidants; and in it he communes with them and with the universe. "Actual poetry," he insists, is "the living speech of person to person"; it "communicates the most intense experiences of very highly developed sensibilities."[2] "A Letter to William Carlos Williams," for instance, conveys such experiences with "enthusiasm and tenderness." It begins:

> Dear Bill,
>
> When I search the past for you,
> Sometimes I think you are like
> St. Francis, whose flesh went out
> Like a happy cloud from him,
> And merged with every lover—
> Donkeys, flowers, lepers, suns—
> But I think you are more like
> Brother Juniper, who suffered
> All indignities and glories
> Laughing like a gentle fool.
> You're in the *Fioretti*
> Somewhere, for you're a fool, Bill,
> Like the Fool in Yeats, the term
> Of all wisdom and beauty.
> It's you, stands over against
> Helen in all her wisdom,
> Solomon in all his glory.
> (*The Collected Shorter Poems*, 193)

17

Just as St. Francis' flesh merged like a cloud with every lover, so does Rexroth's sensibility go out, in this opening stanza of the "Letter," to merge with Williams and other readers. Rather than conceal himself behind an impersonal literary construction—a mask, like Yeats, or an "objective correlative," like Eliot—Rexroth usually stands undisguised. He is the opposite kind of artist from James Joyce, who argued in *Portrait of the Artist as a Young Man,* through his hero Stephen Dedalus, that the true artist, "like the God of the creation, remains within or behind or above his handiwork, invisible, refined out of existence, indifferent, paring his fingernails."[3] Rexroth openly participates in his creation, which is not so much "handiwork" as interaction of poet with subject and readers.

The poetic theory and practice of Kenneth Rexroth, therefore, run counter to the impersonality of much modern literature and criticism, particularly as Eliot theorized in "Tradition and the Individual Talent": "The progress of an artist is a continual extinction of personality.... The poet has, not a 'personality' to express, but a particular medium, which is only a medium and not a personality...."[4] On the contrary, Rexroth's "progress" as a poet has been a continual revelation of personality, the realization of a selfhood. But he is neither exhibitionistic, like Rimbaud or Lord Byron, nor confessional, like Robert Lowell or Anne Sexton. When he writes about himself, he does so objectively, taking himself for granted. Usually, his attention is fixed on other people, or on his relationships with other people, as in the poem to Williams.

In the first stanza we discover him reverently, lovingly searching for an understanding of Williams through comparisons with St. Francis, Brother Juniper, and Yeats's Fool. In the second stanza Rexroth turns out to be so impulsively outspoken in praising his friend that "Your wife thought I was crazy" (193). The blunt spontaneity of such a remark, or of "you're a fool, Bill," or "You're 'pure,' too,/ A real classic" (193), give his abstract thinking a startling intimacy. His diction is "the language really spoken by men," as Wordsworth put it; or in Rexroth's words, "I have spent my life striving to write the way I talk."[5] Even when technical terms from the sciences, philosophy, or theology enter his work, as they frequently do, along with historical and literary allusions, his phrasing is that of living American speech; and his own unmistakable voice comes through. His thinking, no matter how abstract and lofty, emerges from down-to-earth, sensuous experience; and his conversational idiom, tone, and rhythms unite subtle ideas with vivid, evocative imagery.

Although Rexroth does not limit himself to Williams' dictum, "No ideas but in things,"[6] the poets share a devotion to careful perception of the world about them, the world of common humanity: "Dirty rivers, and garbage cans,/ Red wheelbarrows glazed with rain,/ Cold plums stolen from the icebox" (194). This kind of deep perception is what Rexroth calls vision: "Poetry is vision, the pure act of sensual communion and contemplation."[7] He does not mean hallucination or the invention of what does not really exist: "visions are/ The measure of the defect/ Of vision,"[8] he says in a recent poem. Vision is sensing the world in a kind of enlightenment, illumination, the Quaker Inner Light, Zen Satori, awareness that "The holy is in the heap of dust—it is the heap of dust"[9]; or, as William Blake put it, "To see the World in a Grain of Sand/ And a Heaven in a Wild Flower."[10] In vision, the particular is universal, the perceiver is inseparable from the perceived, the poet is pure being, communing with other beings. This interpersonal communion is what Martin Buber calls "I-Thou," a word which, he says, "can be spoken only with the whole being...; as I become *I*, I say *Thou*.... All real living is meeting."[11] In Rexroth's "Letter," for instance, he and Williams unite as an I-Thou; and, in a sense, the poem *is* this communion, this state of mutual being which is the antithesis of the "I-It" condition of estrangement.

Rexroth does not draw a sharp distinction between poetry as verbal communication and poetry as personal vision, or interpersonal communion, which may be silent. Poetry for Rexroth *is* vision, communion itself—silent or spoken. How poetry "works" is a mystery; and the mystery is the condition of quietness to which he responds in Williams' poetry: "Nowadays, when the press reels/ With chatterboxes, you keep still,/ Each year a sheaf of stillness" (194). If we fail to attend to the field of silence from which speech emerges as configurations of sound, we cannot respond to poetry. If we fail to commune with one another, we cannot communicate.

We cannot communicate with one another, therefore, poetically or otherwise, by means of techniques alone. For those to be effective, they must emerge in a field of communion. In Rexroth's "Letter" seven- or eight-syllable lines, one of his frequent prosodic

units, for example, provide an unobtrusive basis for the ebb
and flow of living speech. Three stresses play casually over many
lines; and repetitions of key words such as "I," "you," "like," and
"stillness" not only help shape each stanza but also accumulate
new meanings and intensity as the sentences unwind, some
abruptly direct, some long and sinuous.

In the last stanza there is a remarkable development of the
idea that poetry is not merely a literary game of skill, played
with allusions, forms, and techniques, but is instead an act of
human communion, the source of community. Rexroth imagines
a day when a young woman, walking in a utopian landscape by
the "lucid Williams River," tells her children how it used to be
the polluted Passaic:

> And the
> Beautiful river he saw
> Still flows in his veins, as it
> Does in ours, and flows in our eyes,
> And flows in time, and makes us
> Part of it, and part of him.
> That, children, is what is called
> A sacramental relationship.
>
> (195)

Originating as personal vision which becomes verbal, interpersonal communication, poetry functions as a sacrament, an
act of holy union. Just as the river flows through nature, Williams'
veins, Rexroth's speech, history, his imagined woman and her
children, as well as those of us who read the poem, so all join
in community. The river flows like the Tao, the Way of Lao Tzu,
the Creative Process in which the poet participates. In it, he
creates and celebrates "Sacramental relationships/ That last
always" (195). As Richard Foster has written, this poem is "a
delicately and deeply felt personal tribute—an intimation of the
poet's immortality, a definition of his power and role in the human
community."[12]

Rexroth's poetic theory and practice are therefore religious
as well as esthetic, anthropological as well as psychological—a
philosophical totality which cannot be systematized definitively
apart from the poetry, the vision which is its essence. Light is
thrown on the communal, sacramental function of poetry in his
essay on "American Indian Songs," in which he emphasizes

"the crucial importance of song, and hence the work of art, as the very link of significant life itself, of the individual to his society, of the individuals to his human and nonhuman environment. . . ."[13] And he asserts in *An Autobiographical Novel:* "In the rites of passage—the fundamental activities and relationships of life—birth, death, sexual intercourse, eating, drinking, choosing a vocation, adolescence, mortal illness—life at its important moments is ennobled by the ceremonious introduction of transcendence; the universe is focused on the event in a Mass or ceremony that is itself a kind of dance and a work of art."[14] The experience of transcendence in the key events of life is what Rexroth calls an "anthropological religion" the basis of his poetry. He has written that the anthropologist Edward Sapir was "the only person I have ever met who thoroughly understood what I dreamed of doing with poetry. Out of anthropology, psychology, and linguistics he had developed a kind of philosophy of interpersonal communion and communication."[15] Certainly there is a striking resemblance between Rexroth's thought and that of Sapir, who, for example, defined religious sentiment as "a feeling of community with a necessary universe of values"[16] and who thought that the best poetic style "allows the artist's personality to be felt as a presence, not as an acrobat,"[17] because such artists fit "their deeper intuition to the provincial accents of their daily speech" rather than weave "a private, technical art fabric of their own."[18]

Rexroth's poetic vision, as personal communion, communication, and communal sacrament, however, is developed considerably beyond any influence by Sapir or other thinkers and poets. His poetics defy the categorization of René Wellek and Austin Warren, for instance, who, in *Theory of Literature*, distinguish "intrinsic" from "extrinsic" approaches to poetry, the first being concerned with the poem as a "structure of norms,"[19] and the second covering biographical, psychological, social, and intellectual causes and effects. Rexroth, however, approaches poetry as a total organic process—visionary, communicative, sacramental —in which no aspect is extrinsic: all actuality is part of that process of creation. He is by no means indifferent to prosody and other formal considerations; he is, actually, Classical in his precision. But prosody is subordinate to vision. Poetry turns out to be not an imitation of life but a state of being alive. It is not merely artifice or invention, not primarily a formal, verbal construction, nor an instrument for instruction and pleasure. It is not a means to an end but an end in itself—and not art for art's sake, but being for being's sake. Nor is it simply the expression of ideas and feelings, conscious or unconscious; and it is not regarded by Rexroth as the product of "objective" (biological or social) or "subjective" forces (such as intellect or imagination). Traditional dualisms between life and poetry, poetry and poet, poet and community dissolve in his transcendent view of creative process.

In theory and practice Rexroth is akin to such visionary poets as William Blake, W. B. Yeats, and D. H. Lawrence; like Walt Whitman, the American poet with whom he has the most in common, he is "a kosmos."[20] To understand his originality and the magnitude of his poetic achievement we must consider his work as an integral extension of his personality.

II *The Objectivity of* An Autobiographical Novel (*1966*)

Rexroth's friend Lawrence Lipton has described him as follows:

Think of him, first, as an 11th century figure of a man, scholar, poet, priest, a student from the Latin Quarter out on the town. In his youth, a tramp scholar in the tradition of the goliards, unchurched, unfrocked, unschooled, from whose fingers no book was safe if he needed it, no scholarly discipline too formidable to undertake, no language too arduous to study and master, no way of life too unconventional or too dangerous to sample. A restless experimenter, faithful and faithless by turns to every temptation of the heart and mind, a terror to the Muse herself who is by turns mother, bitch, mistress, faithless whore. And today, in his middle years, a tall greying figure in a ragged overcoat, with a knobbed walking stick and the look of a friendly uncaged lion who delights children and frightens their school teachers. Looks like a younger Albert Schweitzer, talks as I imagine Gilbert K. Chesterton might have talked if he was D. H. Lawrence, lives like St. Francis, and has the reputation of Bishop Golias. Cesar Franck with satyr's hoof showing under a monk's cassock, and blowing a jazz horn. And, by his own description, as American as Mark Twain, as simple as Robert Burns or Tu Fu, as primitive as a Bushman chant, as consecrated and maligned as Peter Abelard.[21]

The more one sees Rexroth, the more believable are Lipton's remarks. Rexroth does have a timeless quality, as if he had stepped out of ancient China, or medieval Europe, or one's home town. He is at once priestly and profane, simple and profound, innocent and sophisticated, gentle and terrifying, erudite and absurd, a philosopher and adventurer, a psychiatrist and a mystic. Who knows what to expect? He may be aloof, sizing up strangers with a sigh as if just waking up. Suddenly, he is animated, intensely involved with those around him, completely outspoken, his conversation becoming spontaneous poetry, polemic, drama, and song.

In *The Dharma Bums,* Jack Kerouac turned Rexroth into Rheinhold Cacoethes, a "bowtied wild-haired old anarchist" who presided over a poetry reading which was the birth of the San Francisco Poetry Renaissance, as Rexroth actually did in 1956. In snide intonations that are precisely Rexroth's, Cacoethes praises characters modeled on W. C. Williams, Gary Snyder, and Allen Ginsberg: " 'I guess the only real poets in the country, outside the orbit of this little backyard, are Doctor Musial, who's probably muttering behind his living-room curtains right now, and Dee Sampson, who's too rich. That leaves dear old Japhy here who's going away to Japan, and our wailing friend Goldbook and our Mr. Coughlin, who has a sharp tongue. By God, I'm the only good one here. At least I've got an honest anarchist background. At least I had frost on my nose, boots on my feet, and protest in my mouth.' He stroked his mustache."[22]

This quotation reflects precisely how Rexroth speaks—bluntly, sardonically, stating opinions as facts and facts as epithets. We hear the same innuendos and intonations in *An Autobiographical Novel,* which he originally dictated into a tape recorder and later transcribed. He notes that this book, which covers the first twenty-two years of his life, was begun as "a gesture of communion with those I love, with my daughters especially. Secondly, of course, it was an attempt to understand myself. I am not so naive as to believe that one reveals oneself by talking about oneself. But possibly out of the narrative a self can be deduced, as Pluto was discovered by an analysis of the perturbations in the orbit of Neptune" (v-vi).

As it turns out, we discover him, in communion with family, friends, and loved ones, acting out an historical role derived from religious and artistic conceptions of prophet and bard, from the American tradition of conscientious dissent and revolt, from the *noblesse oblige* of his parents, and from his own creative imagination. He is not, of course, the role that he acts out; rather, as he tells us, there is "at the final core of self a crystal from which the whole manifold of the personality develops" (v). His adventures are like the sparkling of this crystal at the center of his personality. It is revealed most vividly, I think, in his visions—"momentary flashes of perfect communion with others" (152)—experienced when his mother died (77), again during a visit to a monastery where he very nearly decided to become a monk (334), and in his marriage to Andrée Dutcher at the age of twenty-two, in 1927, at the end of the book: "It is this kind of total identification with one another in which two personalities multiply each other like squared numbers that is the quest of 'spiritual alchemy' and other disciplines of so-called erotic mysticism" (358).

Unless the reader seriously seeks this visionary center of Rexroth's life, he misses the point of the book and of Rexroth's life's work. Leonard Kriegel has condemned him for being "so self-conscious about his emergence as the young artist and Bohemian that he becomes the victim of his life . . . . For this reviewer, at least, that self remains hidden."[23] It is true that many aspects of Rexroth's personality remain mysterious and that his deepest self is revealed more clearly in his poetry than in his prose; but in no sense is he "the victim of his life" It is too bad that Kriegel did not take the modest advice of Sarel Eimerl, who wrote that the book "would not, I think, make suitable reading for the envious, since it is all too likely to depress them, making them brood over how little they know and how much time they've wasted."[24] More important, surprisingly, is an insight in an anonymous review in *Time*: "The author is not the victim of an unsatisfactory love affair with his own personality: he takes himself for granted and spends his space telling about other people, places, and ideas."[25]

Rexroth not only takes himself for granted; he observes himself with the detached interest of a historian or a journalist but with keener psychological insight and artistic control than either of those commonly displays. The book is particularly useful, therefore, not only for its information about his early life, but also for what it shows about his objectivity toward his life and art. By objectivity I do not mean that he is always right or even accurate—and it is likely that biographers and critics will correct statements of fact in the book. I mean that he has that rare ability to look at his own life with the kind of amused interest and detached curiosity that we expect of historians more than from poets, as for example in the following statement: "I was born on December 22, 1905, in South Bend, Indiana. My mother was well past her time. She was sitting in a cabaret, eating breast of chicken on whole-wheat bread with a piece of lettuce and drinking a glass of champagne, as she always did in cabarets, and wondering when I was going to show up when she began to feel labor pains" (19).

Like Defoe, Rexroth has a journalist's dead-pan objectivity which enables him to present this event as if he had observed it; and, throughout those chapters of *An Autobiographical Novel* that cover his ancestors and family before his birth, he seems always to have been present, shrewdly noting everything. He is a master of photographic description, of historical and sociological analysis, and of witty anecdotes and epigrams that establish a convincing sense of fact. The skeptical reader, after putting the book down, tries to untangle the probable from the possible and the possible from the impossible; but the "minute particulars" vividly cohere into a life that defies this kind of analysis, no matter how intelligently conducted. The facts of his life, including fictions more real than statistics, speak for themselves because he writes exactly as he speaks, confident of the objective validity of his personal experience.

His visionary moments, for example, are presented as matter-of-factly as his political adventures in Chicago. We never find passages in the style, say, of W. B. Yeats's *Reveries over Childhood and Youth,* in which fantasy so permeates memory that nothing is certain but the poet's enchantment. Nor does Rexroth fictionalize his life as Marcel Proust and James Joyce did theirs. Nor does he turn his life into apocalyptic rhetoric in the manner of Henry Miller. But, like Miller, he might have quoted, with approval, the following sentence by Ralph Waldo Emerson that appears on the back of the title page of *Tropic of Cancer:* "These novels will give way, by and by, to diaries or autobiographies—captivating books, if only a man knew how to choose among what he calls his experiences that which is really his experience, and how to record truth truly."[26] Miller, uncertain as to "which is really his experience," makes it up as he goes along; but Rexroth, with a clear, confident vision of the past, records "truth truly" without turmoil or confusion. Like a New England Quaker or Transcendentalist, he tells us, in plain speech, about an extraor-

dinary event in a commonplace world: "I was about four or
five years old sitting on the carriage stone at the curb in front
of our house on Marion Street in Elkhart, Indiana. It was early
summer. A wagon loaded high with new-mown hay passed close
to me on the street. An awareness, not a feeling, of timeless,
spaceless, total bliss occupied me or I occupied it completely"
(337-38). If we miss here the subjective complexities of Yeats,
Joyce, Proust, or Miller, we gain, through Rexroth's precise
prose, a realistic sense of the visionary who is in the world but
not of it.

His objectivity is apparent not only in the verisimilitude of
his story telling but also in his attitude toward history, particularly with respect to his family's radicalism. His consciousness
of tradition is certainly as acute and as comprehensive as Eliot's
or Pound's, but it is libertarian instead of authoritarian. Familiar
with many lands and literatures, he has nevertheless never deni-
grated his American experience; like Emerson, Thoreau, Whitman, and Mark Twain, he has accepted that experience, contradictory and painful though it has been, because he has fully
accepted the universality of the self instead of seeking the
authority of an external tradition to discipline the self.

The earliest Rexroths were medieval German intelligentsia,
some perhaps Jewish; and in America the family was a mixture
of Pietists and radicals: "Schwenkfelders, Mennonites, German
revolutionaries of '48, Abolitionists, suffragists, squaws and Indian
traders, octoroons and itinerant horse dealers, farmers in broad
hats, full beards, and frogged coats, hard-drinking small town
speculators, all have gone to make a personality that has proved
highly resistant to digestion by the mass culture and yet, I think,
conservative of the characteristic values of American life rather
than the reverse" (vii).

These values are those of the American struggle for the rights
of conscience, of the revolution for national independence, of
Jeffersonian and Jacksonian democracy, of the free spirit of both
the frontier and of New England Transcendentalism and Aboli-
tionism, of the radicalism of European immigrants, Debsian
Socialism and the Industrial Workers of the World, and the
Populist and Progressive movements for democratic reform.
These aspects of American history are diverse and in some ways
contradictory, but they do share a libertarian spirit that stands
in opposition to militarism, bureaucratic repression, political

persecution, and capitalistic profit-making at the expense of "life, liberty, and the pursuit of happiness." However, we may disagree with Rexroth's interpretation of American history, his concept of the American radical tradition clearly provided him with an objective theater for his personal drama: "It was from several generations who had won all their revolutions and expected to go on winning them that I came" (27).

This tradition developed until World War I, when well-to-do cultured men and women like his parents had a "profound sense of their own responsibility and an awareness of the need for social change" (viii). His father, Charles Rexroth, a pharmacist and businessman of considerable sophistication and charm, was the son of a Socialist plumber and a woman with remarkable gifts as a storyteller, Mary Mohr, who was part Indian and possibly part Negro (3-4). Charles Rexroth was the drinking companion of "James Whitcomb Riley, Eugene Field, Ted Dreiser, George Ade, and others of the first Chicago renaissance, which consisted almost entirely of Indiana-born newspapermen" (53). Charles married Delia (or Della) Reed, who had dropped out of Oberlin College for a brief business career with a suffragette. Delia's father was a friend of Eugene Debs and her mother, a fine folk singer, was descended from an Abolitionist, Indians, and an Indian trader (9-10).

A few months after Kenneth's birth in 1905 the family moved to Elkhart, Indiana, where Rexroth's mother educated him with methods similar to the Montessori system; his father equipped him for scientific experimentation; and an aged Indian companion taught him natural lore (25-39). Kenneth's childhood seems to have been idyllic, and his parents seem to have been a perfect couple until his mother contracted tuberculosis around 1911 and his father took to drink. After a European tour in 1912, they lived in Battle Creek, Michigan, where his father failed in business. In 1916, after moving to Chicago, a series of infidelities and other misfortunes culminated in his parents' separation and in his mother's death. He then lived in Toledo, Ohio, with his paternal grandmother and his father who died of alcoholism in 1918 (80-91).

In *An Autobiographical Novel*, Rexroth displays a cool respect for his father's intelligence and vitality which contrasts with his profound affection for and admiration of his mother, who seems to have been the model for his ideal of the liberated, loving

woman. In a poem, "Delia Rexroth," written a quarter of a
century after her death, he recalls "the ardor of your brain./ And
in the fingers the memory/ Of Chopin études, and in the
feet/ Slow waltzes and champagne twosteps sleep" (CSP, 153).
In another poem with the same title: "I guess you were a fierce
lover,/ A wild wife, an animal/ Mother" (CSP, 186).

His parents had impressed him with a kind of *noblesse oblige*
or "caste responsibility" (37) to the common people. Without
pressuring him, they had provided him with a sense of mission.
Proud of his heritage, which encouraged completely individual
development, he did not have to rebel against it because the
seeds of revolution were in it. Unlike the instinctual radicalism
of mid-century youth in the civil rights, Black power, antiwar,
and student movements, Rexroth's radicalism has never resulted
from an identity crisis. On the contrary, "I have never felt any
inhibition on the development of my personality. . . . I have
always been too busy being a poet or a painter or a husband
or a father or a cook or a mountain climber to worry about my
personality, and this book is my first attempt to consider it at
all" (x). Similarly, he has always felt secure in his heritage—
if not in an America in which people have increasingly been
victimized by technology. His enemy is not the father image
but dehumanizing political-industrial systems based on impersonal, abstract relations among men: "I-It" rather than "I-Thou",
to use Buber's terminology. Rexroth supports youth's revolts
against those dehumanizing systems—Capitalist, Communist, Socialist, Fascist; but he never implies that his own bourgeois
family repressed him: "All those living and dead people provided
me with a kind of family epic in which I thought, still think
of myself, as called to play a role" (ix).

A poem called 'The Bad Old Days" tells how, in 1918, the year
of his father's death, he read Upton Sinclair's *The Jungle* and
saw for himself, in the stockyard area of Chicago, "Debauched
and exhausted faces,/ Starved and looted brains" (CSP, 258).
He took a revolutionary vow that is probably the one of Eugene
Debs that is repeated in *The Dragon and the Unicorn* (CLP,
233):

> While there is a lower class,
> I am in it. While there is
> A criminal element,

I am of it. Where there is
A soul in jail, I am not free.

He soon joined the Industrial Workers of the World, and ever since, his radicalism has remained proletarian but anti-Bolshevik, anarchistic but neither sectarian nor terroristic, always libertarian and humanistic (ANN, 126, 197, 207, 275).

With *The Jungle,* he had read H. G. Wells's *The Research Magnificent,* which had reinforced his family's attitude that he "belonged to a special elite whose mission it was to change the world" (149). According to Rexroth, Wells had secularized "two principles of Judaism: the 'genius,' as prophet, *nabi,* or *vates,* and the source and the final end of creative action in marriage" (97-8); and Rexroth's own radicalism has never been divorced from the prophetic power of love. His parents had embodied, until around 1911, his ideal of marriage. They had carried on a romance with each other which had nurtured his own "infantile matrimony" with Helen Carpenter, when they were six or seven: "This devoted and shared life was for me a foundation for all future experiences. It shaped my method for dealing with life" (50). A couple of years later, when World War I began, he and Carolyn Richter acted out the Oz books in another romance (66), and in Chicago he had a series of love affairs, culminating in his marriage to Andrée Dutcher in 1927.

Meanwhile, he had lived for a couple of years with an aunt on the South Side in James T. Farrell's neighborhood; Rexroth appears in *Studs Lonigan* as a funny boy named Kenny who works in a drugstore.[27] He attended Englewood High School, visited classes at the University of Chicago, and also educated himself in bohemian circles. By 1921, after premiering as "a boy soapboxer, bringing poetry to the masses" (142), he was able to live independently as a journalist, actor, director, painter, and poet (151-76). His reading ranged from Greek and Chinese Classics to "Sandburg, Masters, the Chicago school, the early Imagists, and, in Europe, my father's favorites—Dehmel, Rilke, Verhaeren, the fantaisistes, Jammes. Now I discovered the contributors to Kreymborg's *Others* (what is now the classic generation of American modernists), the new contributors to *Broom* (Hart Crane, Malcolm Cowley, Yvor Winters), and modern French verse, from Mallarmé, LaForgue, Rimbaud, and Apollinaire to the postwar revolution of the Cubist and Dadaist poets.

As might be imagined, this produced an indescribable state of excitement" (122).

Gertrude Stein and T. S. Eliot—especially *The Waste Land*— influenced his early writing, particularly his Cubist and abstract poems, but he soon changed his mind about their work (145 and 257); and, since then, he has attacked the reactionary aspects of Eliot's poetry and criticism. During Rexroth's fifteenth year, especially, "There never seemed time enough for all the thousands of things that absolutely had to be done or written or painted or seen. It seems as though I met most of the important people in America, by my standards, in a matter of three or four years.... It wasn't just the freshness of youth; the century was young, and we were building a new culture and self-educating ourselves—learning by doing" (143).

The two poets who affected him most profoundly during these months were Sappho and Tu Fu. His translation of Sappho's apple-blossom fragment appeared years later at the beginning of his great love poem, "When We with Sappho":

> ... about the cool water
> the wind sounds through sprays
> of apple, and from the quivering leaves
> slumber pours down. ...
>
> (CSP, 139)

During and after translating it, "A whole night was spent in a kind of fury and for the next few days I wandered around in a trance, overcome with joy" (ANN, 154). Even more important was the Chinese poet Tu Fu, "without question the major influence on my own poetry, and I consider him the greatest nonepic, nondramatic poet who ever lived" (319). In what sense are these quiet lyricists compatible with Rexroth's revolutionary outlook? The question is not difficult to answer when we keep in mind that Rexroth's mission since boyhood has been to change the world through love. The sensibilities of Sappho and Tu Fu help form Rexroth's ideal community. The poetry of love prophesies a new humanity.

By age sixteen, Rexroth's fundamental attitudes toward poetry, love, religion, philosophy, and revolution seem to have been formed. He decided to go west, by freight, and he "got/ A job as helper to a man/ Who gathered wild horses in the/ Mass drives in the Okanogan/ And Horse Heaven country" ("A Living

Pearl," CSP, 234). Returning to Chicago, he fell in love again
in 1922, but it was "adult love" this time—with a social worker
named Leslie Smith ("Shirley Johnson") who was several years
older than himself; under her influence, as they read poetry
together, he wrote much of his first long poem, *The Homestead
Called Damascus* (1920-25: see AAN, 191-2, and CLP, 1-36).

In 1926 Rexroth seems to have worked his way to Europe on
a ship and back, meeting many artists and writers there; then
he worked his way to the Far West and Mexico before returning
once again to Chicago (ANN, 341-46). This time he fell in love
with an anarchist painter named Andrée Dutcher. They were
married in 1927 and moved to San Francisco, where he made
his home until moving to Santa Barbara in 1968. Their marriage,
he reports in *An Autobiographical Novel*, was the total realization of all that he had imagined love could offer. A number of
magnificent elegies written some years after her death in 1940
immortalize that remarkable marriage—one, for example, ending:

> We thought the years would last forever,
> They are all gone now, the days
> We thought would not come for us are here.
> Bright trout poised in the current—
> The raccoon's track at the water's edge—
> A bittern booming in the distance—
> Your ashes scattered on this mountain—
> Moving seaward on this stream.[28]

III *Rexroth's Rites of Passage*

The death of Andrée, at the onset of World War II, like the
death of his parents during World War I, was a terrible loss in
which personal grief was deepened by universal catastrophe.
By 1919, he had passed from Blakean innocence to experience,
losing the organic community of family and friends in an optimistic tradition of humane radicalism. In Chicago, he felt after the
war that this tradition still had some life to it, and his participation in the avant-garde community there made him feel that
a new world was imminent. He was briefly encouraged by the
democratic potentialities of the Russian Revolution, but the
brutal authoritarianism of the Bolsheviks horrified him (ANN,
126) as much as the growth of Fascism. In 1927, the year in
which *An Autobiographical Novel* ends, the execution of Sacco
and Vanzetti cast a tragic shadow over his marriage to Andrée

and their move to San Francisco. For Rexroth, the death of the anarchists meant the collapse of postwar optimism. As Frederick J. Hoffman described the case, "It became a critical struggle between right and left, caused explosions in Paris and Zurich, parades and protests in Europe and in South America; it inspired poems, plays, and novels; it served as a crucial test of liberal and radical loyalties."[29] Sacco and Vanzetti, and the significance of their deaths, have haunted Rexroth for decades; his reaction is expressed in some of his finest elegies, such as "Climbing Milestone Mountain, August 22, 1937" (CSP, 89) and "Fish Peddler and Cobbler" (CSP, 319), in which he reflects on "the years/ Of revolutionary/ Hope that came to an end as/ The iron fist began to close." During those happy years the avant-garde expected that soon the lives of everyone would be ennobled. "It will take/ Longer than we expected." he concludes dryly, the truth being, as he fully realizes, that utopia will never come.

Throughout his work, Rexroth has mourned the loss of that utopian hope. He has struggled against despair in a world gone mad, a world in which humane revolutions have been betrayed and perverted, a world in which collectivities of strangers, equipped with runaway technology, push each other toward extinction.

In democratic as in totalitarian societies, he thinks, genuine community is made more and more difficult because people are increasingly alienated from themselves. "The conviction that 'nobody wants me, nobody needs me, nobody knows I exist' may be the birthright of the ghetto, but it is coming to pervade all levels of modern society, even the most productive and favored."[30] Self-alienation has increased in the nuclear age to the point of no return, in his opinion, and he has felt despair as profoundly as have Samuel Beckett, Jean-Paul Sartre, and other major writers.

As in their thought, Rexroth's sense of despair is ultimately metaphysical, founded on a profound sense of mortality in "the night-bound world" (ANN, 319), a universe that is "blind and random."[31] "Part your lips. My dear,/ Someday we will be dead" (CSP, 215), he says in "Rosa Mundi"; and in one of his elegies to Andrée, "The human race sinks towards/ Oblivion" (CSP, 190). Throughout his work he develops the theme that only love, courage, friendship, and loyalty can protect men from an otherwise meaningless universe:

>Homer, and all sensible
>Men since, have told us again
>And again, the universe—
>The great principles and forces
>That move the world—have order
>Only as a reflection
>Of the courage, loyalty,
>Love, and honesty of men.
>By themselves they are cruel
>And utterly frivolous.
>The man who yields to them goes mad,
>Kills his child, his wife or friend
>And dies in the bloody dust,
>Having destroyed the treasured
>Labor of other men's hands.
>He who outwits them survives
>To grow old in his own home.
>>("They Say This Isn't A Poem," Part II, CSP, 313)

His philosophical and poetic efforts to cope with despair are in part derived from the Classical poetry of Greece, Rome, China, and Japan which he has been translating since adolescence; but he is well aware that no return to the past can save the present and future. The problem, as he sees it in his introduction to *The Phoenix and the Tortoise* (1944), is how, "in the face of a collapsing system of cultural values ... to refound a spiritual family" as D. H. Lawrence tried to do. He then describes the process of spiritual development embodied in his poetry.

Implied first, it seems to me, is a fall from Blakean innocence to experience, from the bliss of childhood to "a sense of desperation and abandon in the face of a collapsing system of cultural values" (9). By abandon he seems to mean the *carpe diem* attitude of many of his ironic poems and translations, such as the one called "Several Sources," which ends with the line, "Naked and drunk, we'll find riches in bed" (94). The "recreation of a system of values" is a process which he outlines as follows: "from abandon to erotic mysticism, from erotic mysticism to the ethical mysticism of sacramental marriage, thence to the realization of the ethical mysticism of universal responsibility—from the Dual to the Other" (9). By "universal responsibility" he means "the belief that the only valid conservation of value lies in the assumption of unlimited liability, the supernatural identification of the self with the tragic unity of creative process. I hope I have made it clear that I do not believe that the Self does this by an act of Will, by sheer assertion. He who would save his life must lose it" (9).

Rexroth's outline, however, does not do justice to his spiritual development as we find it expressed in book after book of his poetry. The outline is oversimplified, and the "process" is not a chronological sequence. As we have seen, for example, his family's *noblesse oblige* and Wells's *The Research Magnificent*, among other influences, had brought him to a sense of "universal responsibility" in adolescence; and he had felt "married" even in childhood romances, long before he became concerned about the collapse of Western civilization. The stages of spiritual development are not, therefore, in a linear sequence; they are, instead, states of being through which he has passed and returned at various times of his life, accumulating deeper experience of the problem and the process. His poems may be understood as rites of passage from one spiritual state to another, easing him and his readers through the traumas of change, from despair to love to loss to a larger love, and revealing the mysteries of the universal creative process.

CHAPTER 2

Despair and Revolt between World Wars

REXROTH did not publish his first book, *In What Hour,* until 1940, when he was thirty-five years old; his second was *The Phoenix and the Tortoise* (1944), containing a long philosophical reverie along with short elegies, lyrics, and satires, translations, and imitations; and his third book, *The Art of Worldly Wisdom* (1949), contains some of his earliest poems. They are dated 1920-30 in *The Collected Shorter Poems* (25-78), though he informs us in the Preface to the 1949 volume that most of them were written between 1927 and 1932; and the Epitaph and "In Memory of Andrée Rexroth" must have been written after her death in 1940. Other early poetry, written in Chicago from his fifteenth to his twentieth year, became his first long philosophic reverie, *The Homestead Called Damascus.* Two excerpts, "Adonis in Winter" and "Adonis in Summer," appeared in *The Phoenix and the Tortoise,* but *Homestead* was not published as a whole until 1957 in *The Quarterly Review of Literature,* with excellent notes by Lawrence Lipton. In 1963 it was published by New Directions as Rexroth's ninth book of original poetry; and in 1968 it was included in *The Collected Longer Poems* as the first of five philosophical poems. In *Homestead* the brothers Thomas and Sebastian consider two alternatives to despair: erotic mysticism and heroic martyrdom. But neither is achieved, and the poem ends on a note of philosophical resignation.

Most of Rexroth's other poems of the 1920's are in *The Art of Worldly Wisdom,* in which the most important poem is his second long reverie, "A Prolegomenon to a Theodicy," dated 1925-27 in *The Collected Longer Poems* (37-60). It was originally published, in abridged form, as "Prolegomena to a Theodicy" in *An Objectivists' Anthology* edited by Louis Zukovsky (Le Beausset, Var, France, 1932). The complete version of "A Prolegomenon to a

Theodicy" has been reprinted in *The Collected Longer Poems*. This long poem, Rexroth's most ambitious experiment in literary Cubism, is a kind of "Paradise Regained," beginning with extreme despair and ending with a vision of Christian apocalypse. But the vision seems too literary to ring true, and Rexroth never again wrote anything like it. Among the shorter poems from *The Art of Worldly Wisdom*, reprinted in *The Collected Shorter Poems* (25-78), the most convincing is the sequence of love poems in direct statement, "The Thin Edge of Your Pride" (31-36).

Moving into the 1930's, we discover, in Rexroth's first published book, *In What Hour* (1940), that the poems range in tone from revolutionary optimism to metaphysical despair and in style from Cubism to plain speech. Philosophically, he withdraws from history to nature, from revolution "Towards an Organic Philosophy" (CSP, 101-4).

I   The Homestead Called Damascus

The Homestead Called Damascus (1920-25, published 1957) is a four-part philosophical reverie in lines, generally, of nine syllables, in Rexroth's most musically eloquent style. The narrator, who observes the action as dispassionately as Tiresias in Eliot's *The Waste Land,* begins with a contrast between angels, who are too "modest" and "doubtless" to question mysteries of the universe, and "youthful minds" that

> fret infinity,
> Moistly dishevelled, poking in odd
> Corners for unsampled vocations
> Of the spirit, while the flesh is strong.
> Experience sinks its roots in space—
> Euclidean, warped, or otherwise.
> The will constructs rhomboids, nonagons,
> And paragons in time to suit each taste.
>   (CLP, 3)

The "youthful minds" of the poem are the Damascan brothers, Thomas and Sebastian, who grow from innocence into the experience of despair. They live in "a rambling house with Doric columns/ On the upper Hudson in the Catskills" (3)—the Homestead, which embodies the bourgeois-Christian-Classical tradition in a state of decadence from which they try, in vain, to escape. Their parents might have been imagined by Henry

James or Marcel Proust (18), and their grandfather had stuffed the house with "meaningless/ Bric a brac, the flotsam of India,/ The China trade, and whaling around the poles" (24)—all reminders of imperialistic° glories. Western civilization seems to exist more as a memory, a reverie, than as a reality. In a neighboring mansion, for instance, Sebastian's girl Leslie lives like a Renaissance princess "with her father's falcons,/ Greensleeves and moth breasted birds and pale/ Braided hair, riding side saddle, dressed/ In velvet" (5).

Unsettled by artifice, domesticity, and decadence, the brothers contemplate heroic quests and ancient fertility rites, out of which culture originates; but, fearful of the "little death" of sexual love and the transfiguring death of martyrdom, they never find the grace that came to Paul on the road to Damascus, to pagans in search of Atlantis, or to knights in search of the Holy Grail.

In Part I, the brothers kid each other with allusions to Sir James Frazer's *The Golden Bough;* but the serious reveries of Sebastian, whose "mind was like a dark vault full of/ Spider webs of light" (7), waver between a promise of domestic bliss with Leslie and, at the other extreme, "invisible journeys" to "the martyrdom of arrows" (6) that befell his Christian namesake of the third century. Thomas the skeptic puns his name with Tammuz (Adonis); but, fearful of love, he has nihilistic visions of sin and death; of the devil and Modred, the nephew and murderer of King Arthur; and of "Hakeldama, the potters' field/ Full of dead strangers" (10). The brothers cannot commit themselves to heroic "vocations/ Of the spirit" (3); and the allusive, gnomic style appropriately reveals their unsettled sensibilities.

In Part II, while Thomas embarks on a love quest to New York, Sebastian returns to "A time which he had always known,/ A passing light in which he had/ Always lived" (11); but, recovering from his trance, leaning over a chessboard, he tells himself, "This is getting/ Nowhere" (12); and he reminisces about a black stripper named Maxine, in New York, an earth goddess who "smiles/ A warm domestic smile" (13). But, as if to remind us that Thomas is no Adonis, the narrator breaks in with the brilliant passages reprinted in *The Phoenix and the Tortoise* as "Adonis in Summer" and "Adonis in Winter" (CSP, 159-60):

> The Lotophagi with their silly hands
> Haunt me in sleep, plucking at my sleeve;
> Their gibbering laughter and blank eyes
> Hide on the edge of the mind's vision
> In dusty subways and crowded streets.
> Late in August, asleep, Adonis
> Appeared to me, frenzied and bleeding
> And showed me, clutched in his hand, the plow
> That broke the dream of Persephone.
>
> (CLP, 14)

There follows a vision of geological evolution culminating in "the tangled bodies of lovers/ Under the strange stars" and suggesting the mysteries of creative process, life out of death, to which Sebastian cannot give himself. Nor can Thomas, though he "Peers in the black wounds" of Jesus on Good Friday and "hammers the frame/ That squeezes the will" (17).

Much of Part III is an elaboration of the dilemma between erotic-heroic mysteries involving such fertility goddesses as Persephone, Kore, Theano, and Maxine the Stripper, and, on the other hand, the decadence of domestic bliss. Both alternatives paralyze the brothers—Sebastian, because he fears martyrdom; Thomas, because he doubts that love can be salvation. As a result, each remains alone, dreaming. But in their loneliness, the narrator tries to discover some kind of communion:

> I know this is an ambivalent
> Vicarity—who stands for who?
> And this is the reality, then—
> This flesh, the flesh of this arm and I
> Know how this flesh lies on this bone
> Of this arm, this is reality—
> I know. I ask nothing more of it.
> These things are beautiful, these are
> My sacraments and I ask no more.
> Did I dream about the same woman?
> My fingers twine on themselves and twine
> On the memory of a hand, long
> After that hand. My being is her
> Dream, she has dreamed that journey and dreamed
> That cruel map, that strong manual
> Of demands. I know I am her dream.
>
> (25)

Reality, therefore, turns out to be "ambivalent/ Vicarity"—each person standing for another, interacting in dream, memory, imagination with the other. But this interpersonal communion remains, in the poem, a thought rather than sensuous actuality as in Rexroth's great love poems, such as "When We with Sappho" (CSP, 139); and the tone of this philosophical climax is sombre, not ecstatic, as if the narrator wants more than knowledge.

In the last part, "The Stigmata of Fact," Thomas' skepticism leads him to conclude that "There is no self subsistent/ Microcosm" and that "There is no self subsistent/ Macrocosm either" (32). He means, I think, that there is no autonomous, individual ego; nor is there a God. If reality is "ambivalent/ Vicarity," then each person interacts with all; he cannot transcend the flux. Thomas does not feel totally isolated, but neither does he feel universal. Nor does Sebastian, who concludes that "There is no self that suffers rebirth" (35) and that Maxine's erotic mysteries cannot save him from a "limitless sterile/ Kind of life" (34).

These ideas may be the "rhomboids, nonagons,/ And paragons in time" that the experienced will is said to construct in the opening lines of the poem (3); and the narrator's irony throughout implies that such forms are illusory, concealing a reality that transcends thought. In his "Introduction to the Collected Longer Poems", Rexroth indicates that ideas in his poems are elements in "dramatic dialogue, not the sole exposition of the author, and always they are contradicted by the spokesman for the other member of the polarity. If there is any dialectic resolution, it occurs each time in the unqualified, transcendent experience which usually ends each long poem." *Homestead* ends, for example, as Thomas, in resignation, staring into "the heart of the fire," hears "Bats cry, the creaking of the hundred,/ Tiny, closing doors of silence" (36). Moreover, throughout the poem, visionary passages resolve episodes of philosophical dialectic. After the brothers argue about "Plato and Leibniz,/ Einstein, Freud, and Marx," in Part I, they observe, in meditation,

> The swollen carp ponds, the black water
> Flowing through the clattering rushes,
> And, poised each on one cold leg, two herons,
> Staring over their puckered shoulders
> At a hieroglyph of crows in the distance.
> (5)

This kind of transcendent natural configuration Rexroth later
called after Jacob Boehme, "The Signature of All Things."
Rexroth periodically returns to this kind of visionary experience
after abstract argument; in fact, this oscillation from philosophy
to direct perception is a fundamental characteristic of his style.

Particularly striking in this poem are terms from mathematics
and the natural sciences—"galaxy, dark nebulae"; "space—/ Eu-
clidean, warped, or otherwise"; "rhomboids, nonagons" (3);
"The trigonometry of the rafters,/ The astronomy of the ladders"
(9); "the glacial drift,/ The Miocene jungles, the reptiles/ Of
the Jurassic, the cuttlefish/ Of the Devonian, Cambrian/ Worms,
and the mysteries of the gneiss ..." (14). In later poems, scientific diction includes terminology from the social sciences as well,
making Rexroth, along with Walter Lowenfels, one of the very
few American poets to incorporate modern science into the
language of poetry. As Lawrence Lipton observes, "That constant
shifting from reverie to narration, from the underseas of the
unconscious to geology and archaeology, from inner to outer and
back again, was to become Rexroth's outstanding characteristic."[1]

Lipton—who has known Rexroth since the Chicago years—
has also indicated some of the many influences on the style and
content of Homestead—The Golden Bough and The Waste Land,
James Breasted's History of Egypt and the Arthurian cycle,
Marcel Proust, Rainer Maria Rilke, Guillaume Apollinaire, Francis Jammes, Conrad Aiken, John Gould Fletcher, and others.[2]
And Rexroth modestly admits in An Autobiographical Novel to
being saturated also with The Yellow Book and French poetry,
as well as with Henry James, during the affair with Shirley
Johnson which inspired much of the poem (ANN, 192, 257).
There are also strong overtones of Wallace Stevens in such lines
as "He will know many days of walks in/ Little parks of dead
leaves and sparrows,/ Afternoon with fountains in the haze,/
And the martyrdom of arrows" (6). Nevertheless, Rexroth's distinctive voice predominates; and The Homestead Called Damascus is not only an excellent introduction to his corpus but also
an enduring and unique work of art.

The poem does suffer from obscurity in characterization and
development. Sebastian is no more passionate and no less skeptical than Thomas, and I cannot agree with Lipton that Sebastian
is consistently "voluntary" and Thomas is "involuntary" (43),
though this does seem to have been Rexroth's intention. The

brothers' moods and thoughts are so similar to one another, the vicariousness is so ambivalent, that it is nearly impossible to keep them apart. No doubt they are, as Lipton points out, "two aspects of the poet's personality"—the tendency toward sacrifice and martyrdom, and the restraining tendency of skeptical withdrawal from commitment, with the narrator expressing Rexroth's aristocratic perspective, lofty, wry, and ironic.

The "obscurity" of the poem, like that of *The Waste Land*, is a symptom of original exploration of the spiritual plight of modern man; but, unlike Eliot, Rexroth does not remain distinct from his *personae*: they do not become dramatically objectified, as do Mme Sosostris and the Cockney women in the pub. Rexroth's characters neither act nor argue, perhaps because he could not see his way beyond resignation. The erotic mysteries of Maxine the Stripper and Persephone are sought but not realized in the kind of ecstatic affirmation that we find later in *Beyond the Mountains* and in the best of the love poems. Instead of losing themselves in love or martyrdom, the brothers worry ideas into innuendos until, periodically, they sink into a kind of natural communion—hearing, for instance, the "Voice of speaking leaves and lustral water" (22).

II   The Art of Worldly Wisdom

If in *Homestead* Rexroth searches in vain for perfect love, in the opening poem of *The Art of Worldly Wisdom* (poems from 1920 on; published 1949), an elegy for Andrée, he mourns its loss. Except for this poem, written after 1940, the book consists of work from the 1920's—short poems (in CSP 31-78) and his second long philosophical reverie, *A Prolegomenon to a Theodicy* (CLP, 37-60). He saved some of his earliest poems for his third book, published a quarter of a century after they were written, because, according to his Preface to the 1949 volume (published in a limited edition by the Decker Press in Prairie City, Illinois), "I have withheld them from permanent publication until the time which produced them was no longer an element in the judgment of their value." He seems to have been concerned, not with topicality which might have dated them, but with style and technique: "These poems are not in quest of hallucination. They owe nothing to the surrealism which was coming into fashion when they were being written. One poem is a sort of polemic by example against two leaders of surrealism."

This poem, "Fundamental Disagreement with Two Contemporaries" (for Tristan Tzara and André Breton), begins with a parody containing such lines as "CONCEPTUAL PERSPECTIVE ENGINE/ x y z"; but it later evokes a serious elegiac tone, as in these concluding lines:

> Over the white trees the stars
> iris out in the sky
> metallic breaths cross the air
> and distinct against the dry grass
> the black bears
> the red baboons
> wait, and the little girl
> so pale, so fragile waited
> naked, whispering to herself.
> In the ravines the pilgrims foundered in the mire
> their jaws were broken, they died
> and lay unburied.
>
> (CSP, 54)

Most of the poems in *The Art of Worldly Wisdom,* like this one, are difficult, and the Preface offers an explanation:

They are intended to be directly communicative, but communicate by means similar to those employed by the cubists in the plastic arts or by Sergei Eisenstein in his early great films—the analysis of reality into simple units and the synthesis of the work of art as a real parallel to experience. With the exception of a few philosophical witticisms and a few polysyllables which I would probably not use today, these poems are built of and articulated around elements which are as simple, sensuous and passionate as I could find. The ultimate intent is not merely expressive, or even constructive, but communicative, even didactic. . . .

Technically, I suppose most of these poems represent about as an advanced position as American poetry has taken. I can think only of the poems of Walter Arensburg, Gertrude Stein, Walter Lowenfels, and Louis Zukofsky to compare with them. Of course, similar French poetry has long been accepted by all literate people. They are not "difficult" poems in the sense that the Reactionary Generation which came after them is difficult. There are no Seven Types of Ambiguity lurking in them. Their elements are as simple as the elementary shapes of a cubist painting and the total poem is as definite and apprehensible as the finished picture.   (n.p.)

These remarks deserve to be quoted at length because of the light they throw on Rexroth's most problematic poems. After *Homestead*, which is puzzling but melodiously emotive, much of *The Art of Worldly Wisdom* seems ascetic and antiseptic. "Its special obscurity," asserts Richard Foster, much too harshly, I think, "is roughly like a series of grunts, mumblings, and blurtings heard through a motel wall."[3] And even Rexroth's close friend, Lawrence Lipton, reminiscing about their experiments with automatic writing and hallucination during the 1920's, takes issue with Rexroth's announced intention:

They are good poems, of their sort, but. . . . What is simple, sensuous and passionate about

      As A is.
      A triangular chessboard squared in two tones of gray,
            P to K$_3$, KN x B.
      It's very cold under the table. A cold window.[4]

On the contrary, these lines simply and sensuously communicate elements in the experience of playing chess. Lipton is correct, however, that they are not passionate. And he continues to take issue with Rexroth's announced intention: "Surely, after all these years it is silly to pretend that there weren't times when we were kidding ourselves and kidding each other, just for the hell of it."

No doubt there were such times. But there is plenty of evidence that most of the poems are as serious as Rexroth insists they are. In the earliest extended treatment of Rexroth's poetry, Dorothe Van Ghent has discussed it, along with the poetry of Gertrude Stein and Laura Riding, in terms of dissociation, or abstracting images from the context of personal experience, "just as Alice saw the smile of the Cheshire cat hanging lone and unattended, abstracted from the cat."[5] Paradoxically, abstraction can be sensuous. She finds that in Rexroth's poetry

An enormous enumeration of experiential quantums results, for the reader, in a strong tactile sense. To draw an analogy, it is as if he had been handling the exhibits in a geological or mining museum, his fingers attentive to the varying degrees of roughness, shape, and weight; until, on leaving, he breathed with an assurance of the existence of things—an assurance which Bishop Berkeley could not rob him of. Nevertheless, the rocks and ingots have only disjunctive relationships. They have no metaphysical tie other than that of

existence itself. In other words, they are dissociated. A reader of
the Rexroth poetry who pronounces on its incoherence is in the
same position as one who would feel dissatisfied because the rocks
in the museum did not hang together. His activity would be the
same in either case—a search for a unifying principle.[6]

To Van Ghent, the principle does not lie "*outside* the experiential immediacy of the elements themselves" and is, therefore,
"no different from that reality." It seems to me that this is an
excellent explanation of what Rexroth means by "the synthesis
of the work of art as a real parallel to experience." Van Ghent
has called it "direct sensuous apprehension," borrowing T. S.
Eliot's description of the thought of John Donne, George Chap-
man, and other Metaphysical poets[7]; or, as Eliot said, Dante
"more than any other poet, has succeeded in dealing with his
philosophy, not as a theory (in the modern and not the Greek
sense of that word) or as his own comment or reflection, but in
terms of something *perceived*."[8] She concludes that "In poetry of
this kind, concept has become percept and percept concept."[9]
For instance, she quotes these vivid lines from *Prolegomenon*:
"The burnished ladder of the intellect/ The silver spiral of the
will/ Tense in the telic light" (CLP, 60).
   Surprisingly, Rexroth's Cubist poetry can be passionate, contrary to the opinions of Foster, Lipton, and Van Ghent. Though
Van Ghent asserts that he offers "no emotional attitude toward
his subject matter,"[10] she is, I believe, drawing on one aspect
of objectivist theory that Rexroth repudiates. Certainly the following lines communicate an intense "emotional attitude" as
well as thought; the two, in fact, like concept and percept, are
inseparable:

> Remember that I told you there is nothing to
> Be afraid of
> I said there is nothing
> I said it is a ghost it is a dream a
> Joke an ontological neurosis
> I told over and over
> I said there is nothing
> It is not an abyss
> It is not even
> a pit

                                                               (40)

Here he is concerned, insistent, protective, but desperate: "it is/ So hard to get you to believe me" (42). He tries and tries, but his effort to communicate, to be reassuring, is ultimately futile, for he is "Just born to die/ Nobody will ever know anything about it/ And I have nothing more at all to say" (43).

His despair is in part an awareness of human vanity and mortality, but it is also an awareness that there is nothing beyond: that being is itself nothing, and nothing is itself a dream or joke. That "There is nothing to/ Be afraid of" because "there is nothing" is hardly reassuring. Metaphysical despair is compounded, in fact, by his futile efforts to reassure others. Communication of despair might transcend despair, but he despairs of communicating it. Of course, he does and does not, for his denials of communication are themselves acts of communication.

His despair, moreover, generates the dissociated style, for he cannot organize a poem on the basis of forms—metaphysical or esthetic—in which he does not believe. His poetry is a search for transcendence *within* the flux of personal experience. This is the search that Van Ghent alludes to when she writes that he, more than Gertrude Stein and Laura Riding, stands "in the direct line of the current of anarchy" and "has gone, for subject matter, to value itself."[11] The best evidence for this interpretation is in *A Prolegomenon to a Theodicy,* which she has not analyzed in detail. Of course, Rexroth's vision cannot legitimately be abstracted as a credo or systematic doctrine from the sensuous elements of the poem itself; but the following summary of the poem's "argument" may be helpful in comprehending his approach to the problem of value.

A theodicy is a justification of God's perfection in the light of an imperfect universe. How can God be omnipotent, omniscient, and supremely good if evil exists in man and nature? Rexroth does not offer a logical answer, as Leibniz did in his theodicy; but the *Prolegomenon* communicates the visionary experience without which no theodicy is possible. As we have seen in the lines "there is nothing to/ Be afraid of," the first part of the poem conveys moral and metaphysical despair and Rexroth's frustrating effort to communicate the meaning of nothing.

In the next four parts he explores "ways of being" through "The anagogic eye" (44-45), then suffers through "the winter of the hardest year"—"So many minor electrocutions/ So many slaps of nausea" (45-46)—to the grace of a dawn vision (46-48)

and hymn of praise (48). In Part VI the poet is compared to
a blissful Thomist angel who "is always actually beholding the
Word and the things seen in the Word" (51), but he is tempted
to evade his responsibilities to others that this divine vision
thrusts upon him (52). Character, however, lies in the choice of
"death rather than dishonorable wealth" (55), and in Part IX
there is a Dantean vision of hell:

> The bell
> Too softly and too slowly tolled
> And the first wave was snow
> The second ice
> The third fire
> The fourth blood
> The fifth adders
> The sixth smother
> The seventh foul stink
> And unnumbered beasts swam in the sea
> Some feather footed
> Some devoid of any feet
> And all with fiery eyes
> And phosphorescent breath
>
> (55-56)

Fortunately, from "A mouth filling the sky" is heard "Blessed
are the dead who die" (56); and a visitor, who seems to be a
savior, is admitted by the "bent woman" to whom he had
addressed the opening part of the poem (58). In the final part,
the poet moves climactically toward salvation. First, he is
assured by Aristotle's argument "that which has a natural aptitude
for being moved towards a certain end must needs be able to
reach that end" as well as by the greater wisdom that "An Aristotle was but the rubbish of an Adam and Athens but the rudi-
ments of Paradise" (58). Then the angel Gabriel defeats the
evil spirit, and the poet is blessed by the coming of God, who

> . . . descends five hundred steps
> They hear his breathing secretly
> The murmur of the midnight air
> The unendurable fragrance
>
> (59)

Finally, there is a vision of Apocalypse:

> The ciborium of the abyss
> The bread of light

> The chalice of the abyss
> The wine of flaming light
> The wheeling multitude
> The rocking cry
>
> (60)

The imagery is the most explicitly Christian of any in Rexroth's poetry, and the heavy use of literary tradition, rather than immediate perception, puts a strain on the dissociated empiricism of the rest of the poem. As a way out of despair, he seems to be moving in the direction of Eliot, towards self-sacrificial acceptance of traditional Christian mysteries. But this direction was not continued, as the poems of the 1930's show. *Prolegomenon* is no doubt the least satisfying of Rexroth's longer poems, but it represents his tortured struggle for a faith that transcends the vision of *Homestead,* and certain passages are deeply moving.

Though Cubism is not the style that Rexroth perfected as his most communicative, his experiments of the 1920's were important as a means of discovering new rhythmic possibilities in American speech. "In prosody, and in certain devices of syntax," he writes of the poems in *The Art of Worldly Wisdom,* "they owe much to primitive songs—American Indian, Melanesian, Negro, Negrito, Eskimo, Bushman, *etc.,* and to the study of languages least like the Indo-European group—subjects which greatly interested me then and from which I hoped much new blood could be transfused into English poetry. Medieval Latin poetry, especially the great sequences—in particular of Adam of St. Victor and of Abailard [*sic*]—is another metrical influence."[12]

A thorough examination of Rexroth's prosody and influences on it would require a study much longer than this introduction to his work.[13] He has compared, for example, Rexroth's Cubism with certain chants from the South Seas and American Negro folk songs. For example, we should consider the lines from a Maori chant on the left and Rexroth's on the right:

The thick night to be felt,	The throat of night
The night to be touched,	The plethora of wine
The night not to be seen,	The fractured hour of light
The night ending in death.	The opaque lens
	The climbing wheel

> (46-47)

Lipton does not point out what is perhaps obvious—the liturgical
use of repetition, variation, and parallelism—the basic techniques
of primitive song as described by C. M. Bowra.[14] Less obvious
are Rexroth's subtle patterns of alliteration and assonance:
t's in *throat, night, light* (and the rhyme); *i*'s in *night, wine,
light, climbing; l*'s in *plethora, light, lens, wheel;* and, perhaps
most intricate, the reverberations in *throat* and *plethora*. Van
Ghent has referred to another technique: "The definite article
here . . . is used to build up particularities of existence,"[15] thus
contributing to the rich sense of perceptual immediacy. I might
indicate another technique which may reflect primitive language:
the run-on sentences and phrases that melt into one another, as
in these lines for *Prolegomenon:*

> I think secretly
> Could it have for all the world have been just that
> How have the blanketed eyes
> Sensation drains through the body. . . .
>
>   (41)

Bowra has written that primitive speech "does not need and
does not use highly disciplined sentences, and one sentence flows
easily into another because the functions of words are not fully
differentiated."[16] Rexroth and other participants in "The Revolution of the Word," such as Gertrude Stein and James Joyce,
were attempting to extend the possibilities of language by recom-
bining its elements—in this case, specifically, by juxtaposing
phrases that do not grammatically fit. The clash of structures
and rhythms, in these lines, conveys the painful bewilderment
of metaphysical despair.

    In *The Art of Worldly Wisdom* Rexroth left behind the elo-
quent musicality and dreamy meanderings of *Homestead*. His
syntactic and prosodic experiments convey a harsher, more ascetic
vision. In contrast to the acute dissociation of *Prolegomenon*, the
reveries of Thomas and Sebastian seem dilletantish. The Cubist
experiments produce cadences closer to those of common speech,
though the diction often remains philosophical and literary. In
other words, Rexroth is moving through the Cubist poems to
the direct statement which has become characteristic of most
of his poetry. Perhaps the stylistic development is most apparent
in what seems to me to be the most beautiful poetry in *The Art
of Worldly Wisdom*—a sequence of love poems called "The Thin

Edge of Your Pride." It begins with the lyrical richness of *Homestead*:

> Later when the gloated water
> Burst with red lotus; when perfect green
> Enameled grass and tree, "I most solitary,
> Boating," rested thoughtful on the moated water. . . .
>
> (31)

But the other thirteen sections are personal reminiscences in plain speech, surely more deeply felt and memorable than any of the Cubist poems:

> XIII
> This shall be sufficient,
> A few black buildings against the dark dawn,
> The bands of blue lightless streets,
> The air splotched with the gold,
> Electric, coming day.
>
> . . . .
>
> XIV
> You alone,
> A white robe over your naked body,
> Passing and repassing
> Through the dreams of twenty years.
>
> (36)

III   In What Hour

Rexroth collected his poems of the 1930's in his first published book, *In What Hour* (1940), for which he won the California Literature Silver Medal. These poems are in the various styles in which he had worked during the 1920's. We hear the introspective harmonies of *Homestead* in "The Apple Garths of Avalon," in which Sebastian "strives for swift/ Articulation" (CSP, 111). Cubist experiments continue in "Organon" (113), "Dative Haruspices" (118), and other poems at the end of the book. Most of the poems, however, are in direct statement; and ones at the beginning are oratorical responses to a period of manic-depressive politics. "Gentlemen, I Address You Publicly" (83) is the title of one; others are explicitly anarchist responses to such crises as the execution of Sacco and Vanzetti ("Climbing Milestone Mountain, August 22, 1937," 80), the Sino-Japanese War ("Autumn in California," 93), and the Spanish Civil War ("Requiem for the Spanish Dead," 86).

Without an understanding of Rexroth's development during the 1920's, one is likely to complain about the book, as William FitzGerald did: "As an integrated performance it is less than notable."[17] There are indeed, as FitzGerald pointed out, overtones of Eliot, Pound, Stevens, Crane, Auden—and he might have added Conrad Aiken and Ivor Winters; but he failed to hear Rexroth's distinctive voice and was apparently not amused by his deliberate and brilliant imitations of Auden and Winters (85 and 104). More important, FitzGerald misses the philosophical quest that unifies the book: Rexroth's struggle through desperate historical crises "Toward an Organic Philosophy," as he entitles a crucial poem (101), in which he finds transcendent value communing with the creative processes of nature.

Other critics also missed the point of the book. Horace Gregory and Marya Zaturenska, for instance, wrote in *A History of American Poetry 1900-1940* that *In What Hour* was "regional verse that reflected the charm of the Pacific Coast, and the meditative if somewhat belated contact of a poet with the political and aesthetic 'conversations' of his day."[18] Belated?—after twenty years of radical thought and action in such organizations as the Industrial Workers of the World and the John Reed Clubs?[19] "Conversations" hardly conveys Rexroth's involvement and awareness of current political tragedies and esthetic movements. And the value of the nature poems is not so much that they are regional but that they are transcendental and philosophical. Rolfe Humphries, another condescending critic, wrote: "At his best, he is a simple-minded man with a liking for outdoors . . . . Of this he writes well; his observation is direct and immediately leading him to the true line—'The stone is clean as the light steady as stone' and to happy images. . . . Rexroth's other aspect, the erudite indoor ponderer over many and difficult texts, is less deserving of encouragement. . . . [He should] beat out of his head the idea that the abstractions, whether simple or involute, are the serviceable material of poetic art."[20]

Such dogmatic rejection of abstractions would, of course, legislate against much of Shakespeare, Donne, Milton, and other major poets. Humphries does recognize the brilliance of Rexroth's "minute particulars," but he has no feeling for the movement of sound and idea in abstract passages. We should consider, for example, eloquent lines such as these, from "Value in Mountains":

> Being is social in its immediacy,
> Private in final implications;
> Life is built of contact and dies secretly;
> So existents live in history and die out
> In fulfillment of individuals.
>
> (120)

And if abstract nouns were removed from the following passage from "Ice Shall Cover Nineveh," what would remain of the anguish?

> Speak not let no word break
> The stillness of this anguish
> The omniscience of this vertigo
> These lucent needles are fluent
> In the gold of every memory
> The past curls like wire
>
> (136)

Praise for *In What Hour* has come from Richard Foster, not for the philosophical poems, but for "some memorable and deeply felt articulations of the special sociological traumata of the thirties," particularly the "chillingly prophetic 'The Motto on the Sundial,' a kind of Second Coming."[21] But, unlike Yeats's apocalyptic horror of the "rough beast," Rexroth's mood, in this poem at least, is revolutionary hope. The "voice/ Preparing to speak" (CSP, 88) is the voice of the oppressed and exploited, of whom he wrote in the opening poem of the volume, "From the Paris Commune to the Kronstadt Rebellion":

> They shall rise up heroes, there will be many,
> None will prevail against them at last.
> They go saying each: "I am one of many";
> Their hands empty save for history.
> They die at bridges, bridge gates, and drawbridges.
> Remember now there were others before;
> The sepulchres are full at ford and bridgehead.
> There will be children with flowers there,
> And lambs and golden-eyed lions there,
> And people remembering in the future.
>
> (81-82)

This poem, crucial to an understanding of Rexroth's anarchism, harkens back to an event which has ever since 1921 divided libertarian radicals from totalitarian Communists. The Kronstadt sailors, supporting Petrograd workers who were striking for bread, demanded more representative elections; more freedom of speech, press, and assembly; the liberation of Socialist prisoners; and other reforms. Their demands were attempts to extend the revolution, which had begun to be bureaucratized by the Bolshevik government. They were totally rejected as expressions of "mutiny," and Leon Trotsky, after threatening to "shoot you like pheasants," did just that.[22]

No doubt Communist machinations during the 1930's—in Spain, in the Moscow Trials, in the Hitler-Stalin Pact—caused Rexroth to recall the lesson of Kronstadt; and to show his allegiance with the oppressed against state repression, whether democratic, Communist, or Fascist, he began his first book with this poem. Since boyhood, his revolutionary hopes had periodically risen and fallen, as they continued to do as World War II approached. If the optimism of this poem does not ring true after decades of war, cold war, and betrayed revolutions, we should not necessarily reject the poem, for it remains an eloquent expression of the kind of optimism that was widespread during the 1930's and is also important as one thesis in a dialectic that develops through the book.

The opposite view is expressed in the next poem, "At Lake Desolation," an elegy about mass destruction in which Rexroth sees "Hakeldama, the potter's field,/ Full of dead strangers" (82). Modred had also seen it in *Homestead* (CLP, 10), but in the later poem the vision results from war rather than from a despair that is primarily metaphysical. Pessimism deepens in the next poem, "Gentlemen, I Address You Publicly" (CSP, 83), in which the poet recommends suicide; but he begins to discover meaning in death in "Hiking on the Coast Range" (84). On the anniversary of the San Francisco General Strike, he finds "the source of evaluation" in "This minimal prince rupert's drop of blood." Only in the mystery of such sacrifice is "The measure of time, the measure of space,/ The measure of achievement" (84). Sacrifice, then, is an essential element in the creative process of the universe. In "Requiem for the Spanish Dead," for instance, reflecting on them "clotted with blood" as he walks in the night, he hears emigrants singing for a dead child as "Orion moves westward across the meridian,/ Rigel, Bellatrix, Betelgeuse, marching in order,/ The great nebula glimmering in his loins" (86-87). Similarly, as in "Climbing Milestone Mountain, August 22, 1937," he associates the deaths of Sacco and Vanzetti with the permanence of mountains (90); in "Falling Leaves and Early Snow," men fall like leaves as "The year fades with the white frost/ On the brown sedge in the hazy meadows,/ Where the deer tracks were black in the morning" (109); and, in "August 22, 1939," certainly one of the most poignant poems in the book,

> we made four major ascents,
> Camped for two weeks at timberline,
> Watched Mars swim close to the earth,
> Watched the black aurora of war
> Spread over the sky of a decayed civilization.
> These are the last terrible years of authority.
> The disease has reached its crisis,
> Ten thousand years of power,
> The struggle of two laws,
> The rule of iron and spilled blood,
> The abiding solidarity of living blood and brain.
>
> (98)

The "solidarity" in which he puts his faith is not based on an economic class but on flesh-and-blood community. Throughout *In What Hour,* he moves from the horror of modern history, from the tragic destruction of impersonal masses, toward the mysterious processes of nature. In "Another Early Morning Exercise" (92-93) and in "New Objectives, New Cadres" (95-96), ideologies fail to justify suffering, much less end it; so he turns to mountains and stars in "Toward an Organic Philosophy" (101-4). In this fine poem, in which references to human struggles are conspicuously absent, solitude in the mountains evokes a profound awareness of "the chain of dependence which runs through creation" (quoted from Tyndall, 104). As Rexroth communes with the universe, "The sky comes close to my eyes like the blue eyes/ Of someone kissed in sleep" (102).

But such sensuous awareness of organic harmony did not satisfy Rexroth's philosophical inclinations. His longings for abstract comprehension produced "Ice Shall Cover Nineveh," which he lists as one of the reveries to be considered with the longer poems.[20] The title is derived from a legend that the Gurgler Glacier once covered Nineveh because the people were too miserly to feed a hungry pilgrim who was said to be one of the Magi. The poem opens with a familiar scene of mountain solitude: "Distant on the meridian verges/ And the soft equinoxes calling" (130). But the calm is upset by the thought that death is inevitable, for both individuals and civilizations: "Neither fortified in dolmen nor reclined/ In tumulus shall white throat and quick hand hide/ Nor eye escape the rasp of powdering time" (131). Who can make sense of such loss? And who can justify or transform it into value? In trying to cope with inevitable annihilation, Rexroth proposes that we "Discover the apostleship of diffidence" (133), a kind of "natural piety"—to use Wordsworth's term, which Rexroth might find too simple—through which he discovers an enduring glory in the eternal patterns of the universe:

> Only the inorganic residues
> Of your aspiration remain
> Combed over by constellations
> Vivisected by blades of wind
> Fear no more the chill of the moon
> No brisk rodent fear
> Nor thirty years' dreams of falling
> For frozen on the fixed final summit
> Your mineral eyes reflect the gleaming
> Perpetual fall of a cube of singular stone
> Coursing its own parabola
> Beyond imagination
> Unto ages of ages
>
> (135)

To find transcendence in the natural process of creation out of destruction is a chilling "solution" to the problem of value, but it offered Rexroth a firmer foundation than the Christian apocalyptics we find in his *Prolegomenon*. We find the Damascan brothers achieving a kind of natural communion in *Homestead*, but theirs is a mood of resignation because of their failures in love. In "Ice Shall Cover Nineveh" and in "Toward an Organic Philosophy," despite an underlying tone of tragic acceptance, there is a more positive sense of transcendence through natural communion. Transcendence through love with another person is not a major theme of the book; but his second wife, Marie, is referred to in several poems. The only love poem is "An Equation for Marie," and it is full of metaphysical conceits atypical of Rexroth's best, most personal work.

In my opinion, the best poem in *In What Hour*, stating Rexroth's position as a poet of conscience more directly and memorably than any of the others of this period, is "August 22, 1939," one of several memorials for Sacco and Vanzetti: "What is it all for, this poetry,/ This bundle of accomplishment/ Put together with so much pain?" (97). His answers are traditional, learned from Li Po and Dante. Poetry, he says, reveals:

> The pure pattern of the stars in orderly progression,
> The thin air of fourteen-thousand foot summits,
> Their Pisgah views into what secrets of the personality,
> The fire of poppies in eroded fields,
> The sleep of lynxes in the noonday forest,
> The curious anastomosis of the webs of thought,
> Life streaming ungovernably away,
> And the deep hope of man.
>
> (97)

This hope, faint though it may be, can emerge only from an acceptance of death, loss, and destruction as aspects of the universal process of creation. "Values fall from history like men from shell-fire,/ Only a minimum survives,/ Only an unknown achievement" (98). Insofar as poetry is a vision of loss, flux, or dying, it reveals value.

CHAPTER 3

Love as Universal Responsibility

URING the 1940's Rexroth perfected his poetry of direct statement. He turned away from Cubist experiments and the political rhetoric of the 1930's and in two books—*The Phoenix and the Tortoise* (1944) and *The Signature of All Things* (1950) —he searched for the "integral person" who, through love, discovers his responsibility for all in a world of war, cold war, and nuclear terror. The communion with nature which he had celebrated in "Toward an Organic Philosophy" (CSP, 101) continues to be fundamental; but his great achievements of this decade are poems that affirm more convincingly than ever the transcendent power of personal love. This achievement grows painfully out of painful crises such as the death of Andrée in 1940 and divorce from his second wife, Marie, in 1948. A deep, elegiac tone pervades his work.

The Phoenix and the Tortoise, Rexroth's second book to be published, is much more coherent in style and theme than his first. For it he received a second California Literature Silver Medal Award. The title poem, his third long philosophical reverie, written during World War II (1940-44), has been reprinted in *The Collected Longer Poems* (61-92) after *Homestead* and *Prolegomenon*. In the 1944 volume, it is followed by a section of lyrics, elegies, and satires that have been reprinted, newly arranged, in *The Collected Shorter Poems* (137-72). And the third section of the book consists of "Translations and Imitations" of Chinese, Latin, and Greek poetry, chosen "to show forth a sense of desperation and abandon," as he explains in his introduction to the volume (9).

The introduction is a kind of manifesto of Rexroth's personal mission in a collapsing civilization. As we have seen in discussing his "Rites of Passage," he moves from despair through the "I-Thou" of erotic mysticism to sacramental marriage, in which

56

he discovers "universal liability, the supernatural identification of the self with the tragic unity of creative process" (9). In his poetry he attains—not by ego or will, but through the grace of imagination—communion with nature and those he loves; and, in a transcendent community of love, he discovers himself as a being responsible for all.

This Personalism shapes two important essays of the decade— his introductions to the *Selected Poems of D. H. Lawrence* (1947) and to his anthology, *The New British Poets* (1949), a book which he worked on while traveling in Europe on a Guggenheim Fellowship in 1948 and 1949. Also in 1949 his third book of poems, *The Art of Worldly Wisdom*, containing the early poems which we have already discussed, was published, and he married Marthe Larsen—his third wife—who, the next year, gave birth to their daughter Mary. That same year *The Signature of All Things*, his fourth book of poems, appeared, containing some of his greatest short poems of visionary love.

I   The Phoenix and the Tortoise

"The Phoenix and the Turtle", attributed to Shakespeare, celebrated the erotic union of opposites in which "Single nature's double name/ Neither two nor one was called" and "Either was the other's mine."[1] In the mysterious union of lovers Rexroth found a solution to the problem of human identity and responsibility posed in the title poem of his second book, *The Phoenix and the Tortoise* (1944). It was, however, not so much the Elizabethan poet as Plutarch who presented him with the title and "problem." At the beginning of the poem Rexroth contemplates dying creatures on the seashore and geological strata recording time that "flowed eventless as silt"—

> And I,
> Walking by the viscid, menacing
> Water, turn with my heavy heart
> In my baffled brain, Plutarch's page—
> The falling light of the Spartan
> Heroes in the late Hellenic dusk—
> Agis, Cleomenes—this poem
> Of the phoenix and the tortoise—
> Of what survives and what perishes,
> And how, of the fall of history
> And waste of fact—on the crumbling

> Edge of a ruined polity
> That washes away in an ocean
> Whose shores are all washing into death.
>
> (CLP, 64)

What, if anything, transcends time, which seems to be a geological, biological, and historical process of degeneration? In
war, Western civilization seems to be perishing as Greek civilization had perished. Out of the "waste of fact," how can human
values survive? Is it possible that destruction is part of a creative
process? As in "August 22, 1939" (CSP, 97) and in other poems
in his first book, he finds value in the sense of loss; his philosophizing emanates from his elegiac brooding; transcendence lies in his
poetic response, rather than in doctrinal answers. His method is
Socratic, doubting each answer that he discovers. At one point,
for instance, he seems to be agreeing with Aristotle that

> Poetry is more philosophic
> Than history, and less trivial.
> Poetry presents generalities,
> History merely particulars.
> So action is generalized
> Into what an essential person
> Must do by virtue of his essence—
>
> (65)

But he remarks later, "How comfortable, and how verbal" 67)—
as if formulations reveal less truth than the search for it. There
is "Always the struggle to break out/ Of the argument that
proves itself . . ." (68). And the struggle leads him to a critique
of "Aristotle's recipe book" which "Neglects to explain why
tragedy/ Is tragic, the hero, heroic" (70).

Condemning theories of personality and history in which
reason, ego, and will are basic, he discovers the transcendent
person through sensuous vision. He prepares Passover "supper
on the anniversary/ Of the white gift of sacramental flesh" (66),
after which he and his wife make love. Later, in half-sleep,

> I see in sudden total vision
> The substance of entranc'd Boehme's awe:
> The illimitable hour glass
> Of the universe eternally
> Turning, and the gold sands falling
> From God, and the silver sands rising

> From God, the double splendors of joy
> That fuse and divide again
> In the narrow passage of the Cross.
>
> (72)

This passage seems to me to be much more convincing than the apocalyptic conclusion of *Prolegomenon*. Both are derived from literary sources; but the imagery in the earlier poem, such as "The ciborium of the abyss" and "The bread of light," seems cerebral and artificial, whereas he has thoroughly absorbed and transmuted Boehme's vision, conveying it as an authentic "re-vision" in cadences of his own distinctive voice. His presence is felt throughout *The Phoenix and the Tortoise;* but it is hard to find, as a personal voice, behind the Cubist configurations of *Prolegomenon;* and in *Homestead* he had projected aspects of himself as the three *personae,* the Damascan brothers and the narrator.

Part II of the title poem of *The Phoenix and the Tortoise* is more indignant than the first, more explicitly anarchistic in the tradition of Piotr Kropotkin, Mikhail Bakunin, the Industrial Workers of the World, and Jesus Christ: "The State is the organization/ Of the evil instincts of mankind." "War is the health of the State? Indeed!/ War is the State." "Liberty is the mother/ Not the daughter of order." (74-76) And:

> The World, the Flesh, and the Devil—
> The Tempter offered Christ mastery
> Of the three master institutions,
> Godparents of all destruction—
> "Miracle, Mystery, and Authority—"
>
> (74)

After the contemplative tone of Part I, these epigrams strike like missiles. Extreme shifts of style from philosophical abstractions to sensuous imagery, from rhetoric to elegy, cohere in the "essential person" of the poet. Rexroth comes through, in this poem, as a uniquely thinking, passionate human being—Aristotle's "concrete universal," a person who, in the depths of his own suffering and struggle, reveals humanity. I do not mean that Rexroth, like Walt Whitman, preaches his own universality. Rather, it is revealed through the range of Rexroth's thought and perceptions, his feeling and imagination. Far from being arrogant about his own virtues and achievements, he appears in this poem

as a man who is uncertain of all "solutions." Nearing sleep in
frosty moonlight, he remembers heroes, martyrs, and poets whose
personalities transcend the waste of history:

> Nicias in rout from Syracuse;
> Scarlet Wolsey splendid on the Field
> Of the Cloth of Gold; More on trial;
> Abelard crying for that girl. . . .
>   (78)

Waking beside his wife at dawn, in Part III, he continues to
rage against history, whose "goal is the achievement/ Of the
completely atomic/ Individual and the pure/ Commodity rela-
tionship" (80-81)—"I-It" supplanting "I-Thou." He berates intellectuals who sell themselves to the state. "Salvation equals
autonomy," as all major religions have taught, in vain (82). He
ironically contrasts the Sophist "Hippias and Socrates/ Contend-
ing for the title/ Of Most Autonomous Greek"—Hippias "with
the most matériel," the most salable skills, "And Socrates, playing
practical jokes on the imperium" (82-83). The dominant tone is
that of tragic recognition of historical depersonalization. Of what
use is thinking? As his wife sleeps on, he suspects that "her
dreams measure the hours/ As accurately as my/ Meditations
in cold solitude" (85). Somehow, beyond thought, he is united
with her, "Caught in the turning of the seasons" (85).

Finally, in Part IV,

> It is Good Friday Morning;
> Communion has past to Agony
> And Agony is gone and only
> Responsibility remains. . . .
>   (88)

He thinks of such "self-determining persons" as D. H. Lawrence
and Albert Schweitzer; and, recalling a glorious vision of a rain-
bow and crosses in the sky, reported by Whymper the explorer
on the Matterhorn, he feels that the light of dawn focuses through
him to infinity.

Only through loss is transcendence possible; only through
destruction is creation possible:

> This is the minimum negative
> Condition, the "Condition humaine,"
> The tragic loss of value into

> Barren novelty, the condition
> Of salvation; out of this alone
> The person emerges as complete
> Responsible act—this lost
> And that conserved—the appalling
> Decision of the verb "to be."
> Men drop dead in the ancient rubbish
> Of the Acropolis, scholars fall
> Into self-dug graves, Jews are smashed
> Like heroic vermin in the Polish winter.
> This is my fault, the horrible term
> Of weakness, evasion, indulgence,
> The total of my petty fault—
> No other man's.
>
> And out of this
> Shall I reclaim beauty, peace of soul,
> The perfect gift of self-sacrifice,
> Myself as act, as immortal person?
>
> (91)

The question is unanswered; and the poem ends as his wife, nude and singing, comes toward him from the breakers.

Erotic and matrimonial mysticism as an alternative to despair is suggested in various passages about his wife, Marie, as well as in such generalizations as "History/ Is the instability/ Of the family constellation" (80) and "Babies are more/ Durable than monuments" (86). But the emphasis of the poem is not so much on the duality of lovers as on the "integral person," responsible for all. Such a person finds transcendence in the tragic process of creation, manifested, paradoxically, by the destructive passage of time—historical, biological, geological, astronomical. Out of the "waste of fact" value emerges—through human communion. Rexroth's attention to death, his consciousness of natural destruction and of total war—in the images of the drowned Japanese sailor discovered by children (64), for instance, or the "Shadow of a camouflaged cruiser" (86)—causes despair but also overcomes it. Communing with beings that pass away, he attains transcendence with them, in the universal process of creation, for he is "the self-determining person,/ He who discriminates structure/ In contingency" (89).

I have quoted from the poem at length in order to exhibit the stylistic range of the poem, as well as its ideas. The syllabic lines of elegiac direct statement are brilliantly controlled, their tones varying from gentle lyricism to belligerent rhetoric. Neither the elusive musicality of *Homestead* nor the harsh Cubism of *Prolegomenon* was adequate for the kind of philosophical communication that he achieved in *The Phoenix and the Tortoise*. Having perfected this style, he continued to use it for his next long poem, *The Dragon and the Unicorn*, as well as for many short poems.

II *Shorter Poems and Translations*

The second part of the 1944 volume contains shorter poems, and the third consists of translations and imitations. The original poems celebrate erotic mysteries, for the most part; and the first of these, "When We With Sappho" (CSP, 139-42), is in my opinion his greatest love poem—not counting the passionate dialogue of his four verse plays, *Beyond the Mountains*. In *An Autobiographical Novel* he described how, as a boy translating Sappho's "Apple Orchard," he had received "those first kisses of the muse"—"the first intimation I had of what it meant to be a creative artist" (154). "When We With Sappho" begins with his translation:

> ". . . about the cool water
> the wind sounds through sprays
> of apple, and from the quivering leaves
> slumber pours down. . . ."

> We lie here in the bee filled, ruinous
> Orchard of a decayed New England farm,
> Summer in our hair, and the smell
> Of summer in our twined bodies,
> Summer in our mouths, and summer
> In the luminous, fragmentary words
> Of this dead Greek woman.
> Stop reading. Lean back. Give me your mouth.
> Your grace is as beautiful as sleep.
> You move against me like a wave
> That moves in sleep.
> Your body spreads across my brain
> Like a bird filled summer;
> Not like a body, not like a separate thing,
> But like a nimbus that hovers
> Over every other thing in all the world.

> Lean back. You are beautiful,
> As beautiful as the folding
> Of your hands in sleep.
>
> (139)

The intensity of direct address mounts from the melodious languor of the opening lines, with their hypnotic repetition of "summer," to the startlingly dramatic "Stop reading. Lean back. Give me your mouth." Few love poems in English, and none that I know of in American literature, communicate more passionately and sensitively the nuances of erotic bliss. In the alchemy of love, each body, uniting with the other, becomes a "nimbus" over the world; each self, merging with the other, becomes universal, timeless, immortal as Sappho, whose ancient world returns in the next stanza. Then, as "The sweet virile hair of thunder storms/ Brushes over the swelling horizon," passion increaseas sharply: "I will press/ Your summer honeyed flesh into the hot/ Soil, into the crushed, acrid herbage/ Of midsummer" (140). Afterward, they rest. They read to one another, again savoring Sappho's poem, "hidden from fact and history" (141). Finally, in silence, their bodies fall away as the sun falls away, "As we, with Sappho, move towards death" (142).

In the act of love they transcend mortal flesh, uniting with each other and the universe. The moment of union is timeless; and, though they fall from it back into time and mortality, the poem saves their union from dissolution. As Richard Foster has written: "The words of Sappho, the effulgence of midsummer, the deep, still lateness of afternoon, and the slow, full passion of lovers lying together in the orchard of a ruined New England farm fuse, as in the momentum of a completely counterpointed piece of music, into a love poem of astonishing immediacy."[2]

The poem is not *about* the event but is itself an act of visionary communion which recurs whenever the poem is read imaginatively. As such, it is a kind of ritual, a sacrament. Throughout the second section of the book many other fine poems "celebrate the daily/ Recurrent nativity of love,/ The endless epiphany of our fluent selves,/ While the earth rolls away under us" ("Lute Music," 143). In "Floating," for instance, the moment of transcendence occurs as he says

> Move softly, do not move at all, but hold me,
> Deep, still, deep within you, while time slides away,

> As this river slides beyond this lily bed,
> And the thieving moments fuse and disappear
> In our mortal, timeless flesh.
>
> (144)

Mortal flesh becomes "timeless" in the act of love and in the poem. And there are many others celebrating the mystery of "one doubled thing" in "one fused lust" ("Inversely, As the Square of Their Distances Apart," 148).

In "Incarnation" (162), however, union with his wife is achieved at a distance, in "a vision of you/ More real than reality." Climbing a mountain he sees, through "whirling iris perfume" of a waterfall at sunset, his wife far below; he sees her so vividly he seems to touch her:

> Your thigh's exact curve, the fine gauze
> Slipping through my hands, and you
> Tense on the verge of abandon;
> Your breasts' very touch and smell;
> The sweet odor of sex. . . .
>
> (162-63)

Union at a distance is possible because vision is sensuous, the body is spiritual, a creative process permeates the universe, joining all beings together. One common manifestation of this process is "the year's periodicity" ("Precession of the Equinoxes," 154), "The annual and diurnal patterns" ("We Come Back," 163):

> Now, on this day of the first hundred flowers,
> Fate pauses for us in imagination,
> As it shall not ever in reality—
> As these swifts that link endless parabolas
> Change guard unseen in their secret crevices.

These lines are an excellent example of discriminating "structure/ In contingency" (CLP, 89), of recognizing patterns of eternal return. Richard Foster has called the poem beginning with these lines "one of the fullest and most delicate moments I have found in any poet";[3] and surely the image of the "swifts/ Plaiting together the summer air all day,/ That the bats and owls unravel in the nights" is one of the most beautiful expressions of organic transcendence in American poetry.

Two excerpts from *Homestead,* "Adonis in Winter" and "Adonis in Summer" (CSP, 159-60), included in *The Phoenix and the*

Tortoise, also derive from "diurnal patterns," the first being an ironic treatment of the Persephone myth, and the second presenting the "geologic ladder," a favorite subject of Rexroth's. Whether the patterns are astronomical, geological, seasonal, or erotic, they manifest creation out of destruction and patterns of permanence in a universe of flux. The configurations emerge from a field of multiplicity, separation, alienation, decay, and death—the "nightbound world" (ANN, 319): the ruined farm of "When We With Sappho," for instance. Or, in "Another Spring" (CSP, 145), "Moments that should last forever/ Slide unconsciously by us like water." Or in "Habeas Corpus" (146),

> You have the body and the sun
> Brocaded brown and pink naked
> Wedded body, its eternal
> Blood biding the worm and his time.
>
> (146)

And in his adaptation of Martial (XII, LII, 164), he foresees his own death:

> This is your own lover, Kenneth, Marie,
> Who someday will be part of the earth
> Beneath your feet; who crowned you once with roses
> Of song; whose voice was no less famous
> Raised against the guilt of his generation.
>
> (164)

There are a few satires in the second section of the book— "Gas or Novacaine" (151), denouncing the impotence of intellectuals in the face of atomic disaster; "Incense" (167) and "A Neoclassicist" (167), aimed at a silly female mystic and a priggish lecher—but most of the poems are elegiac. I have previously referred to the elegies to his mother ("Delia Rexroth," 153) and to his first wife, Andrée (154, 166). There are also a couple of war poems—"Strength through Joy" (156) and "Un Bel di Vedremo" (158)—that remind us of his denunciations of history and the state in the long reverie, the completion of which is celebrated quietly in the final poem of Part II, "Past and Future Turn About" (168).

In this poem, he and Marie return in autumn to the beach where once again he contemplates dying sea creatures and geological records of millennia of life and death. Neither will

nor reason can create meaning or find transcendence in this
universe of perpetual flux. "The Cross cannot be climbed upon./
It cannot be seized like a weapon/ Against the injustice of the
world" (169). He doubts all doctrines, including his own formulations: "Christ was not born of Socrates" (169); salvation comes
not from reason but from "innocence and humility" (169). And
yet sacrifice guarantees nothing. If anything lasts, it is patterns
of things that change and disappear:

> Autumn comes
> And the death of flowers, but
> The flowered colored waves of
> The sea will last forever
> Like the pattern on the dress
> Of a beautiful woman.
>
> (172)

The translations and imitations in Part III of the 1944 volume
reveal the tradition from which Rexroth derived his perspective
on permanence and change and also his style of direct address,
of person-to-person intimacy and immediacy. Unfortunately,
these poems have not been included in a section in *The Collected
Shorter Poems*, though they have been reprinted in various volumes of Rexroth's translations. (The pagination here refers to
the 1944 volume.) The following poem by Tu Fu shows why
this Chinese poet has been, in Rexroth's words, "the major influence" on his poetry (ANN, 319):

> It is late in the year;
> Yin and Yang struggle
> In the brief sunlight.
> On the desert mountains
> Frost and snow
> Gleam in the freezing night.
> Past midnight,
> Drums and bugles ring out,
> Violent, cutting the heart.
> Over the Triple Gorge the Milky Way
> Pulsates between the stars.
> The bitter cries of thousands of households
> Can be heard above the noise of battle.
> Everywhere the workers sing wild songs.
> The great heroes and generals of old time
> Are yellow dust forever now.
> Such are the affairs of men.

> Poetry and letters
> Persist in silence and solitude.
>
> (92)

On the other hand, many of the poems that follow, from Roman sources, are full of fierce invective which Rexroth adapted for his own use in denouncing history, the state, and the silliness of intellectuals, among other evils. In *"Marcus Argentarius,"* for example, "In Hell the learned sit in long rows saying,/ 'Some A-s are not B-s, there exists a not B.'/ You'll have time to grow wise in their company" (93). And we have also the adaptation from Martial which Rexroth has addressed "To a Revolutionary Surrealist":

> Don't pay any attention
> To this synthetic spectre
> Raving interchangeably
> About the revolution
> Of the exploited masses
> And the diseased gyrations
> Of his sensibilities.
> He was a bride last night.
>
> (96)

But the volume ends on a note of gentle resignation, with epitaphs from the Greek Anthology, such as one by Meleager that concludes: "Let the earth/ Which has borne us all, bear you,/ Mourned by all, gently forever" (98). And the book ends with this poem by Crates: "Time's fingers bend us slowly/ With dubious craftsmanship,/ That at last spoils all it forms" (100).

The book is beautifully organized, just as Rexroth describes it in his introduction. The third section reveals perfectly the cultural decay, despair, and resignation which the modern world, like the ancient, is experiencing. From this state of being Rexroth moved into the erotic and ethical mysticism of the short poems of the second section. And the long poem beginning the book embodies his idea, and experience, of love as universal responsibility. The book is a rare achievement.

III *Lawrence, Thomas, and Other British Poets*

Three years after *The Phoenix and the Tortoise*, Rexroth published his first major essay, the Introduction to the *Selected Poems of D. H. Lawrence*,[4] to whom he had dedicated his own poems. Lawrence's erotic and matrimonial mysticism is an important clue to Rexroth's; for he tells us that "Hardy was a major poet. Lawrence was a minor prophet" (4). "Like Blake and Yeats, his was the greater tradition." "From one point of view," he continues, "Lawrence is the last of a special tradition that begins with St. Augustine and passes through Pascal and Baudelaire amongst others, to end finally in himself" (4). What Rexroth seems to mean is that Lawrence worked his way through the sexual guilt that has tormented Western man—"the insane dynamic which has driven him across the earth to burn and slaughter, loot and rape" (5). Lawrence "exorcised that demon," transcending that tradition of depravity, through acceptance of his erotic attachment to his mother in such poems as "Piano" (55), "Silence" (50), and "The Bride" (49)—which remind us of Rexroth's own sensuous elegies to his mother, remembered as "a fierce lover,/ A wild wife, an animal/ Mother" ("Delia Rexroth," CSP, 186; see also 153).

Both Rexroth and Lawrence return to the creative mysteries of the universe that have been obscured by centuries of Christian taboos. Like Blake, they discover the universal in the "minute particular," because it manifests the eternal process of creation. As Rexroth explains in his Introduction, "From this time on"— when Lawrence wrote the poems to his mother—"Lawrence never lost contact with the important thing, the totality in the particular, the responsibility of vision. . . : the blue vein arching over the naked foot, the voices of fathers singing at the charivari, blending in the winter night, Lady Chatterley putting flowers in Mellors' hair" (6).

The most intense examples of erotic vision, however, he points out, are in Lawrence's Rhine Journey poems—"December Night" (70), "New Year's Eve" (70), "Coming Awake" (71), and "History" (73), about which Rexroth writes so eloquently: "Reality streams through the body of Frieda, through everything she touches, every place she steps, valued absolutely, totally, beyond time and place, in the minute particular. The swinging of her breasts as she stoops in the bath, the roses, the deer, the harvesters, the hissing of the glacier water in the steep river— everything stands out lit by a light not of this earth and at the same time completely of this earth, the light of the Holy Sacrament of Marriage, whose source is the wedded body of the bride" (11).

Though Rexroth modestly omits mention of his own love poetry, its outstanding qualities—in "When We With Sappho" (CSP, 139) and in "Floating" (144)—are precisely those of Lawrence's. In the latter poem, for instance, are such passionately perceptive lines as "Take me slowly while our gnawing lips/ Fumble against the humming blood in our throats." Occasionally there is stylistic imitation, as in "Runaway," which begins, "There are sparkles of rain on the bright/ Hair over your forehead" (142); but usually the similarities are because both poets share visionary and sacramental experiences of erotic union.

It is sad that Rexroth's second marriage, to Marie, ended in divorce in 1948. "I would not have you less than mutable," he had written in the dedicatory poem in *The Phoenix and the Tortoise* (CSP, 137); and, in "Inversely, As the Square of Their Distances Apart" (148-49) and in many other poems, the transcendent union of lovers is followed by "The inescapable vacant/ Distance of loneliness" (149). In a sense, love is eternal—while it lasts; the loss of it is an immortal pattern of poetry.

In the same year, traveling in Europe on a Guggenheim Fellowship, which was renewed the next year, 1949, he edited an anthology, *The New British Poets*. In his Introduction, his remarks about the swing from "the gospel of artistic impersonality" to "the person to person responsibility of artistic creation," following the Spanish Civil War, throw light on his own development. In other words, he finds in British poetry from 1937 to 1949 a growing affirmation of the same values expressed in his own poetry of this period—personal integrity, direct communication, an anarchistic sense of apocalypse, the transcending union of love, and a visionary involvement in creative process. His comments on Dylan Thomas, for example, extend his insights into the creative process: "Most of his early poetry is about the agony and horror of being born and of childbirth. The substance of Rank's *The Artist* is that the artist is, psychologically, his own mother. Few have ever realized this as thoroughly and as violently as Thomas. For him the crucifixion and the virgin birth are one simultaneous process, archetypes of the act, or rather catastrophe, of the creative consciousness" (xix).

Such a passage—and there are others in the Introduction as suggestive as this one—helps us understand Rexroth's elegies to his mother and his interest in Lawrence's poems to his mother as expressions of the poet's discovery of himself as his own creator.

His person, the deeper self, is, in a sense, the creative process of the universe. Whatever it experiences, therefore, is total.

IV   The Signature of All Things

Rexroth's fourth book of poetry, *The Signature of All Things*, (1950), contains no long poem. Instead, there are, according to his grouping, poems and songs such as the great title poem—actually a sequence of three—and "Lyell's Hypothesis Again"; elegies, such as those to his mother and first wife; verse letters to William Carlos Williams and William Everson, who later became Brother Antoninus; translations and imitations of Italian, Chinese, Greek, and Latin poets; and epigrams on love and war, poetry and human follies, philosophical dilemmas and "the touch of/ A calm I cannot know," suggested by "a picture/ Of the vase containing Buddha's relics" (89). In his introduction, pointing out the lack of political and protest poems (such as those in *In What Hour*), he states that "These are all simple, personal poems, as close as I can make them to integral experiences. Perhaps the integral person is more revolutionary than any program, party, or social conflict" (9). Modestly, he refers readers to "better statements" of his "religious anarchism," or Personalism, in the work of Martin Buber, Albert Schweitzer, D. H. Lawrence, D. T. Suzuki, Piotr Kropotkin, the Gospels, Buddha, Lao Tzu, Chuang Tze, and Jacob Boehme, the seventeenth-century mystic, from whose book, *The Signature of All Things*, Rexroth took the title for his own.

"'The whole outward visible world with all its being is a signature, or figure of the inward spiritual world," wrote Boehme: "whatever is internally, and however its operation is, so likewise it has its character externally; like as the spirit of each creature sets forth and manifests the internal form of its birth by its body, so does the Eternal Being also."[5] This doctrine of correspondences is familiar to readers of Blake, Emerson, Whitman, and other nineteenth-century poets; Joyce's "epiphanies" are a twentieth-century manifestation. For Boehme, a man is a signature of God; he is "God's masterpiece, a living emblem and hieroglyphic of eternity and time. . . ."[6]

Boehme's most profound ecstasy occurred as he "gazed fixedly upon a burnished dish which reflected the sunshine with great brilliance"[7]—to which Rexroth alludes in his poem called "The

Light on the Pewter Dish" (209). Boehme reported that "In this light my spirit suddenly saw through all, and in all created things, even in herbs and grass, I knew God, who He is, how He is, and what His Will is."[8] Through Rexroth's book of poems the light of divine love streams through the universe—most brilliantly in the first poem of the sequence called "The Signature of All Things." In this poem as he reads Boehme's book by a waterfall, golden laurel leaves

>   float
> On the mirrored sky and forest
> For a while, and then, still slowly
> Spinning, sink through the crystal deep
> Of the pool to its leaf gold floor.
> The saint saw the world as streaming
> In the electrolysis of love.
>
> (177)

And as the hours pass,

> I think of those who have loved me,
> Of all the mountains I have climbed,
> Of all the seas I have swum in.
> The evil of the world sinks.
> My own sin and trouble fall away
> Like Christian's bundle, and I watch
> My forty summers fall like falling
> Leaves and falling water held
> Eternally in summer air.
>
> (177)

In the other two poems of the sequence, divine light, "the electrolysis of love," appears again and again—in the "blotched and cobwebbed light" of a moonlit oak grove where black and white Holstein heifers lie under "huge trees rooted in the graves" of Indians (178), and in the brilliant correspondence between "swaying islands of stars" and "quivering phosphorescence" of a rotten log he had chopped for kindling: "And all about were scattered chips/ Of pale cold light that was alive" (179). In this sequence, thought and perception are united in poetic vision. There is no distinction between what Rexroth sees, what he thinks, and what he says. "This is a poetry of reality," Gordon K. Grigsby has written, "a poetry of the world that exists beyond metaphor and opinion—ultimately—all poetry and all language."[9]

Another way of saying the same thing is that in this kind of poetry, words are signatures that refer, or evoke, a silent presence of the poet as universal person.

In "Monads," on the other hand, Rexroth thinks *about* what he sees—sunlight shining through an aquarium filled with dino-flagellates. These biological monads remind him of Leibniz' elemental souls, each of which mirrors the universe, of Lucretius' atoms, and of "meteoric dust" (176).

But the poem remains more speculative than visionary. As in much of *The Phoenix and the Tortoise,* Rexroth is puzzling over the nature of reality rather than seeing it in a flash. When he does see it, there is a sense of total communion with another person. In the poem beginning "A fervor parches you sometimes" (entitled "Between Myself and Death" in the *Collected Shorter Poems,* 175), he tells Marie that "the wheel of change stops" as "pride lights your flesh—/ Lucid as diamond, wise as pearl—/ . . . . And the beautiful fire spreading/ From your sex, burning flesh and bone. . . ." Coming at the beginning of the book, these lines suggest that the divine love-light is Eros. When it goes out, it leaves "signatures" which reveal the universal process of creation.

In "Lyell's Hypothesis Again," he compares his ego—"bound by personal/ Tragedy and the vast/ Impersonal vindictiveness/ Of the ruined and ruining world"—and said, 'This far/ And no further.' And spoke thereafter/ In the simple language of stone" (180). And in the second half of the poem he notices

> Tiny red marks on your flanks
> Like bites, where the redwood cones
> Have pressed into your flesh.
> You can find just the same marks
> In the lignite in the cliff
> Over our heads.
>
> (181)

These marks are "ideograms/ Printed on the immortal/ Hydro-carbons of flesh and stone," signatures to be read by the poet, who must observe them as precisely as a geologist. Though Rexroth cannot renounce the search for a coherent theory of reality, he discovers reality, not through abstract thought, but through sensuous perception.

It is no wonder that Selden Rodman has praised Rexroth's

"delight in what used to be called Nature, and the choice of the appropriate word to express that delight. Whether it is hawks 'playing together on the ceiling of heaven,' deer 'bouncing in and out of the shadows like puffs of smoke,' an engorged creek which 'roars and rustles like a military ball.' "[10] But he failed to grasp the depth and meaning of Rexroth's poetry, which is not nature poetry so much as philosophical vision. Rodman's review ends with a strange admonition to "ignore momentarily the pursuing Furies and his own imagined shrinkings under their lash."[11] He seems to be telling the poet to turn away from the reality of "Ten years of wars, mountains of dead"—as Rexroth puts it in "Me Again" (CSP, 109). Though *The Signature of All Things* appeared five years after World War II, several poems are written during the war—the adaptation of "Ausonius, Epistle VII" (200) being the most explicit. We would expect a wise critic to read such poems, in time of peace or war, as elegiac reminders of historical tragedy, instead of urging the poet to avoid his responsibility to the suffering of humanity. The book more than accomplishes what Rexroth set out to do—reveal the "integral person" in a universe in which creation is a tragic process, manifested in warfare as well as in geological strata.

CHAPTER 4

Drama and Dialectic of Community

NOTING the absence of a long philosophical poem from *The Signature of All Things*, Rexroth stated in his introduction to that volume: "I have been working on one for several years, but it is not ready for publication. Meanwhile, I have found it interesting to subject my philosophical opinions to the test of dramatic speech. At present, you can read in periodicals and anthologies the series, *Phaedra, Iphigenia at Aulis, Beyond the Mountains*, Nōh plays on classical themes in which I hope some of my ideas have found a more direct expression than philosophical elegy affords" (9).

The long philosophical poem, *The Dragon and the Unicorn*, was published as his fifth book of poetry in 1952, the year after the plays were collected.[1] Actually, there are four plays, the third being retitled *Hermaios*. It and the fourth, *Berenike*, are grouped as *Beyond the Mountains*, which also serves as the title for the whole collection. I believe that Rexroth's poetic, philosophical, and visionary powers reach their epitome in this tetralogy. "It is a feat of no mean significance to raise the colloquial tone to lines of tragic significance," William Carlos Williams wrote. "I have never been so moved by a play of verse in my time."[2] Thanks to the precisely passionate direct statement —in lines varying, usually, from seven to nine syllables—the characters are genuinely heroic wtihout ever being bombastic. Iphigenia, Hippolytus, Phaedra, and others achieve transcendence through the mysteries of erotic union and sacrificial death. In no work does Rexroth communicate more profoundly the meaning of love as universal responsibility and the integral person as the source of community.

"The plays and *The Dragon and the Unicorn* complement each other and could profitably be read together," Rexroth wrote in his note on the plays (9). His fifth book of poetry, written

74

between 1944 and 1950 and published in 1952, consists of his fourth long philosophical reverie. In style and content it resembles *The Phoenix and the Tortoise* more than the other longer poems; but, whereas the earlier poem is a meditation by the Pacific Ocean, where Rexroth temporarily withdrew from civilization during World War II, *The Dragon and the Unicorn* is based upon his postwar travels across America, through England, France, Switzerland, Italy, and back to America, from New York to San Francisco. In this poem, he emerges more clearly than in any of his other work as a man very much in the world but not of it, as a contemplative who is deeply involved erotically, intellectually, and artistically with many kinds of people in many nations. His tone ranges from erotic lyricism to indignant pathos aroused by scenes of poverty and despair, from savage denunciations of rich American tourists, effete artists, capitalism, and the bureaucratized Left to lofty speculations concerning "The insoluble problems—/ The order of nature, the/ Ego and the other, the/ Freedom of the will. . ." and many other problems, culminating in his idea of Reality as a "Community of lovers" (CLP, 172-3).

I   Beyond the Mountains

Though Rexroth's characters are derived from Euripidean tragedy, the form of his plays is more Japanese than Greek. They compare very well with Yeats's *Plays for Dancers*, which were also influenced by Nōh drama. Yeats's description of Nōh, in "Certain Noble Plays of Japan," helps us understand Rexroth's drama:

No "naturalistic" effect is sought. The players wear masks and found their movements upon those of puppets: the most famous of all Japanese dramatists composed entirely for puppets. A swift or a slow movement and a long or a short stillness, and then another movement. They sing as much as they speak, and there is a chorus which describes the scene and interprets their thought and never becomes as in the Greek theater a part of the action. At the climax, instead of the disordered passion of nature, there is a dance, a series of positions and movements which may represent a battle or a marriage, or the pain of a ghost in the Buddhist Purgatory.[3]

Generally, this description holds for Rexroth's plays. Dances express, for instance, the sexual ecstasy of Phaedra and Hippolytus; and in *Berenike* "The Huns rush on and dance a wild, acro-

batic military dance" (190) that expresses the collapse of Classical
civilization. In the plays there are two choruses, the first consisting of a young prostitute and beggar whose curious resemblance to various heroines and heroes is a reminder that
tragic figures emerge from, and return to, the community of
common people. At the conclusion of the tetralogy, departing
from the principle that the chorus does not become "a part of
the action," the beggar changes roles with Menander, and the
prostitute with Berenike. The second chorus, throughout, consists
of four musicians who act also as "mob, commentators, prop
men, and sound effects" (14).

Another important quality of Nōh found in Rexroth's plays
is *yūgen*, a term derived from Zen Buddhism and defined by
Arthur Waley as "'what lies beneath the surface'; the subtle,
as opposed to the obvious; the hint, as opposed to the statement. . . . The symbol of yūgen is 'a white bird with a flower
in its beak.' "[4] Rexroth's dialogue is philosophically rich, always
suggestive, never prosaic; his ideas are at once clear and evocative; and *yūgen* characterizes his exploration of the mysteries of
communion. "We meet and touch and pass on," the First Chorus
says in *Berenike,* "As log meets log in mid-ocean" (189).

Rexroth tells us in his note to the plays that they are concerned
"with the same root types, the same dramatic figures; with the
relation of the person to the world of occurrence—of what might
and what does happen" (9). One type is the destructive man of
the world, such as the usurper Demetrios, who kills the utopian
Hermaios; Theseus, who cynically lets Athens sicken while he
visits Persephone in Hades; and Agamemnon, who sacrifices his
daughter Iphigenia, despite his knowledge that victory over
Troy will not be worth the price. Transcending the world of
injustice, on the other hand, are certain women of enchantment
identified with "Artemis, the huntress of souls,/ The healer and
the avenger,/ The lady of the moon filled lake" (32). Iphigenia,
the most saintly of all Rexroth's characters, persuades Agamemnon to sacrifice her to Artemis because of "the purity of the
deed" (74). Tarakaia, the mistress of Hermaios, goes to her
death as bravely as she slaughtered Huns. Phaedra seduces her
stepson Hippolytus, but her conscience drives her to suicide. And
Berenike seduces the usurper Demetrios in order to stab him
in vengeance. Though their motives are mixed, they all act out
of conscience shaped by reverence for Artemis.

Their male counterpart is the visionary who, usually enamored of the Artemis-personalities, tries to detach himself from the world but does so with varying degrees of uncertainty, like Sebastian and Thomas in *The Homestead Called Damascus.* Hippolytus is torn between the human love of Phaedra and the divine love of Artemis. Achilles is guilt ridden because of his consuming love for Iphigenia. Hermaios idealistically wants to create a Greek utopia as a last refuge from Romans and barbarians. And Menander tries to escape responsibility for the death of his mother by believing that "My acts/ Will be only images of acts" (155). The men are less charismatic than the women; but their moral dilemmas, resolved only in tragic catastrophe, make them more humanly sympathetic.

Some of Rexroth's characters—Phaedra, Hippolytus, Iphigenia, for instance—are derived from Euripides, but they are transformed with the kind of moral clarity that we associate more with the characters of Sophocles. In *Classics Revisited,* Rexroth made a distinction between the two playwrights that is most helpful in understanding his own plays:

The tragedies of Sophocles are conflicts of fate and personality, will and time. The tragi-comedies of Euripides are confusions of luck and individuality. Egocentric people are caught in the falsehoods, not the truths, of time—misrepresentations, mistakes, confusions, doubles, incognitos. They play their roles in picturesque, romantic landscapes, quite unlike the classic parks of Sophocles or the immense vistas of Aeschylus. Their morality is a deliberate, ironic imitation of the real Heroic Age *ethos*—pluck, gang loyalty, sexual passion. Suffering never ennobles them, as it does the Greek gentlemen of Sophocles, but only coarsens still more the bourgeois sensibility beneath the heroic mask—to an appalling degree in *Orestes, Medea, The Trojan Women* or Pasiphaë's speech in a fragment of a lost play.[5]

In Rexroth's plays, cynical men of the world such as Demetrios, Theseus, and Agamemnon are treated as Euripides would have presented them—as mock-heroic imitations. Their motives are debased by their vulgarity, sentimentality, and callousness. On the other hand, he treats women of Artemis such as Iphigenia and Phaedra, and their lovers Achilles and Hippolytus, as Sophocles would have conceived them—as ennobled by their suffering. Their fate is their responsibility, not the result of an external cause of catastrophe. In moral triumph and physical defeat they struggle in communion with others. Their love is universal; their sacrifice renews community.

Phaedra, the first play of the tetralogy, depends upon Euripides' *Hippolytus*; but Rexroth has radically transformed the main characters and has made explicit the elements of fertility ritual from which Greek tragedy emerged: "Crops wither and men quarrel," says the Second Chorus. "Something is wrong with our queen" (16). While King Theseus commits adultery with Persephone in Hades, Phaedra rages against the Greeks who savagely killed her father, King Minos, smashed Crete, kidnapped her, and made her a princess—"a kind of whore. . ./ If it weren't/ For us there'd be no history" (27); for in sexual reproduction her flesh becomes "immortal, passing/ From dying spirit to spirit" (24). Enraged, she performs the Minotaur dance, the fertility rite on which Cretan civilization depended; but alone, she is powerless, mad, sterile. Meanwhile, her stepson Hippolytus, abandoning "the duty of a prince,/ To open bellies for new/ Infant armies to march out" (18), has become an ascetic seeking visions of Artemis.

In Euripides' play, a Nurse-confidante to whom Phaedra admits her love for Hippolytus, betrays the secret to him, and he self-righteously rejects her and is falsely condemned by his father. But Rexroth drops the Nurse; and, perhaps influenced by the possibility of a lost earlier version by Euripides in which Phaedra directly proposes to Hippolytus,[6] he brings the couple face to face, Phaedra aroused, and Hippolytus falling into her arms as if she is Artemis. "They dance the dance of the world/ That they alone rule over"(36)—the universe of erotic union. When they part, she predicts, "We will have to pay for this./ Life, like any property,/ Is acquired by theft" (38). He is optimistic, but she knows that Theseus will find them out: "The world's destructive children/ Dictate their own terms to fate./ It's people like you and me/ Fate traps and the Furies haunt" (40). They are not simply victims of vengeful Aphrodite, as in Euripides' version, but are doomed by their sense of responsibility.

Hippolytus momentarily regrets this mortal love which has prevented him from attaining immortal union with Artemis but Phaedra persuades him that he has attained vision in her arms, and there is more than a suggestion that she is the goddess incarnate. When she asks him, "If you saw her, are you sure/ You'd recognize Artemis?" (35), he turns dead white. But even

after accepting her love, he has difficulty accepting the consequences. She insists that "vision costs"... : "There's no other
way—/ Vision—evisceration" (42). He does not understand; and,
as her speech becomes more paradoxical, he wants "the ordinary
bliss/ Of a human woman's body,/ Not a wedding with black
nothing" (44). Suddenly, losing her sense of responsibility, she
proposes that they escape to a utopian colony in Italy; but he
renounces political leadership and accepts their love, here and
now, regardless of consequences. She agrees, with a cruel
paradox:

> It's now or never? This now
> Is never. Kiss me. Take me.
> You can have the power now
> To take me beyond return.
> But what returns if you do,
> Is your responsibility.
> Now do you know what I mean?
> (47)

And he replies:

> I understand you. I can see
> Fire spray from our union and burn
> Down the world, and burn us with it.
> Let it burn. We are all burning.
> (47)

They drink sacramental wine from "the brain pan of Minos" (48),
they dance again, and the Chorus sings a final hymn to their
transcendent love: "Worlds bloom in their flaming hair" (49).
They have entered the tragic mystery of creative process.

When Theseus returns from Hades, Phaedra commits suicide,
and Hippolytus courageously confronts him, expecting horror
and wrath. But, unlike the suspicious, grief-struck, vengeful
Theseus of Euripides' play, Rexroth's character is a "man of the
world" who, far from being upset by incest and adultery, tells
his son that he "planned it that way" to satisfy them during
his absence (52). Euripides has Hippolytus, a self-righteous
virgin condemned to unjust banishment, smashed in his chariot,
chased by a bull; whereas Rexroth's hero is trampled to death by
the bull on which his father had ridden from Hades. At the end,
instead of Artemis' bringing Theseus to enlightenment, remorse,
and final reconciliation with his dying son, as in the original,

Rexroth's Theseus, incapable of moral responsibility, wonders, "Why should things like this/ Have to happen to me all the time?" (55).

The First Chorus, however, understanding the moral irony, says of the lovers:

> Her love was not strong enough,
> And her vanity took flesh.
>
> His frail pride could not understand
> That lewd hungry animal.
> . . . .
> Each sinned with the other's virtue.
>   (55)

Or, as the Author's Note informs us, "Phaedra and Hippolytus achieve transcendence but are destroyed by impurity of intention" (9): the animal in each falls for the divinity of the other. Nevertheless, they achieve transcendence through perfect erotic union and sacrificial death—the unfulfilled dreams of the Damascan brothers in *Homestead*. Phaedra is the wiser of the two, taking full responsibility for her own acts and weeping not "For our own private misery,/ But for the chaos of the world" (34). Hippolytus, however, grows in consciousness and responsibility to the point where he can say, "We are all burning" (47), and he can face Theseus.

The characters in *Iphigenia at Aulis,* the second play, are wiser than those of the first. Agamemnon is a more sensitive man of the world than Theseus; Achilles, more aware of the consequences of love than Hippolytus, escapes his tragic death; and Iphigenia, as Rexroth describes her in his introduction, "marches straight to transcendence," her motives being the purest of any in the tetralogy.

In Euripides' *Iphigenia at Aulis*, her father Agamemnon invites her and her mother Clytemnestra to come from Argos to Aulis, where the Greek ships are becalmed, for the ostensible purpose of marrying Achilles; actually she is to be sacrificed to Artemis, who will blow the ships to Troy. When Iphigenia discovers his real purpose, she at first pleads with him, for "It is better that we live ever so/ Miserably than die in glory"; but later, inexplicably, she resolves to die for Greece so that "I, savior of Greece,/ Will win honor and my name shall be blessed."[7] In

Rexroth's version, however, she has initiated the idea of her sacrifice, but for three months her father has resisted her offer. Loving her more than his Euripidian counterpart, he is, in fact, her lover, and he tells her, "You're worth more/ Than Helen, more than any victory." Nevertheless, as a man of the world who believes that "We are bound by the power of dead acts" (67), he allows her to persuade him. Ironically, she uses arguments that he used in Euripides' play. Ironically also, he is more concerned about his own guilt than about her death: "You've no right to treat me as a means/ To your salvation. I've myself to save" (81). Meanwhile, she has achieved perfect union with Achilles, and they celebrate their love in some of Rexroth's most passionate lines. She tells him:

> I have no
> Being but what fills me with you,
> Like a mirror filled with the sun.
> I see world upon world in me,
> Like diamonds in that sunlight.
>
> (70)

And he:

> As I look in your entranced eyes,
> I see mirrored there a glory
> Beyond the illusion of the world.
> I merge with its mirrored image,
> And pass from glory to glory.
>
> (85)

Nevertheless, their love cannot prevent her from sacrificing herself—not in order to insure a Greek victory, but for "the purity of the deed" (73). As the Chorus tells her,

> You will act past consequence,
> Choose past possibility,
> Know past the meaning of truth,
> As you have desired past act.
>
> You know what you are doing.
> Only the beautiful know.
>
> That is a definition
> Of beauty, perhaps the best.
>
> (76)

In her acts of love and sacrifice, she becomes "the Queen of
Heaven/ And Earth, the Living Artemis" (80). She dances
ecstatically, erotically, with Agamemnon, who knows that she
will die, and with Achilles, who, despite his wisdom, believes that
they can be reunited after the war. As Agamemnon kills her
offstage the Chorus concludes the play:

> The knife is black with her blood.
>
> Heaven has taken her. She
> Has gone into the bright world.
>
> The flames crawl over Troy's walls.
> Asia falls into ruin.
> Aeneas and Odysseus
> Wander, lost in a new world.
> Helen dies in a brothel.
>
> (91)

These lines are reminiscent of Yeats's at the beginning of
The Resurrection:

> Another Troy must rise and set,
> Another lineage feed the crow,
> Another Argo's painted prow
> Drive to a flashier bauble yet.[8]

And, like Yeats's play, the last two by Rexroth—*Hermaios*, taking
place in the last outpost of Greek culture "on the eve of the first
night of the Christian era" (95), and *Berenike*—ritualize the
transition from pagan to Christian culture. Yeats "saw a staring
virgin stand/ Where holy Dionysus died. . ." (364). Rexroth's
Choruses, at the beginning of *Hermaios*, prophesy:

> The goddesses that loved the Greeks
> Sprang forth from the thundering sky,
> Or rose, wet with love, from the sea.
> The desert will give up this god,
> A baby of blood in the dark,
> A burning baby from the ice.
>
> . . . .
>
> The lily of a myriad years
> Is a baby whose extended
> Arms branch into infinity.
>
> (101)

But it is the chaos of fire and blood, rather than the lily of resurrection, that Rexroth, like Yeats, emphasizes in his plays. Hermaios Soter, utopian ruler of the last independent Greek city state (in Bactria, Afghanistan), agrees with the Magi that a new god is being born; but, instead of accompanying them to Bethlehem, he has been trying to appease a gang of Huns in order to preserve this bastion of Classical culture. Betrayed by them, he has temporarily fought them with the help of his heroic mistress, an Indian named Tarakaia, who worships Artemis in visionary trances. His wife and sister, Kalliope, urges him to escape to Rome, but he proudly lashes imperial decadence in one of Rexroth's most cutting satires: "What have I to do/ With a world of rhetoricians,/ Pederasts and worshippers of Caesar?" (125). Instead, he proposes to make 'A perfect city here. Plato's dream./ The city of the Sun.../...a city of brotherly love" (126). Kalliope and her brother and lover Demetrios seem to agree with him, but they treacherously lure to their deaths him and Tarakaia, who go with foreknowledge and dignity as smooth-talking Demetrios takes over.

"In *Hermaios* and *Berenike* all the characters are caught in the web of cause and effect," Rexroth tells us in his note; "and the reader will have to judge for himself who achieves transcendence, how, and to what degree" (9). It seems to me that Hermaios achieves it by virtue of his utopian commitment; but it is limited by ego and will, as was Classical culture. He is the last Greek humanist; he dies for nothing new. Tarakaia is more enigmatic. Despite her heroism, she asks the Chorus, as she faces death, "Help me. I am weak and afraid" (138). Artemis cannot help her; and Tarakaia in her helplessness has more compassion for others than Hermaios, who goes to his death certain that he has made the wisest possible decision. "As I watch the fierce stars shining/ On all the twisting roads of pain," she says, "I know it is not I alone,/ Caught in the freezing of the year" (138). This hint of universal sympathy gives her transcendence. Despite her ferocity in fighting the Huns, she has the kind of sensibility that might have responded to Christianity.

In the final play, *Berenike,* the Chorus, watching over the bodies of Hermaios and Tarakaia, expresses the doctrine of total responsibility that Rexroth develops in *The Phoenix and the Tortoise* and in *The Dragon and the Unicorn*: "The evils of the world are the/ Reflexions of the owner of/ That world" (150).

Hermaios' daughter, Berenike, vows vengeance against the usurpers Demetrios and Kalliope; but her brother Menander, who is even more passive and withdrawn than Hippolytus, tells her that she is "snarled in the web of cause./ I only want to turn no more/ On the turning wheels" (152). Berenike, who is even more willful than Phaedra, replies:

> You are blind.
> The door to inaction is called
> Action, and the gate of action
> Is called inaction. You cannot
> Find bliss by dropping your eyelids.
>   (154)

She begs him to use her to avenge their father's death:

> I want to be
> Like a straw cart loaded with fire,
> A vehicle which perishes
> As it runs. I am yours to burn.
>   (157)

He denies that he has will, judgment, fire, being. She persists, dancing with swords, joining with him ecstatically as Phaedra and Hippolytus danced, but he continues to be passive. So she turns to Demetrios, and, seducing him, she stabs him as they dance. He dies cynically, and she foresees the inevitable end of herself and the Classical world: "New love. New death,/ My sweet brother" (174). He nevertheless still refuses to act, and the Chorus agrees that

> We act in the world of illusion
> Where action is busy with means.
> In the world of reality
> The single act is its own end.
>
> . . . .
>
> There are no things in the real
> World. Only persons have being.
>   (181)

As Berenike dances, the Chorus announces the end of the Greek era and sings the first Delphic hymn. Sword in hand, Menander confronts Kalliope but does "not dare to take vengeance" (186). Nevertheless, accepting full responsibility for her crimes, she knows that history, or fate, will move the sword from his hand to her heart (188); and it does just that as the Chorus announces the birth of Christ. Acting in spite of himself, Menander loses the moral purity he had tried so carefully to preserve. She achieves transcendence by taking responsibility for her acts, whereas he does not even die. Instead, through complicated dance movements at the finale of the tetralogy, they take the places of begger and prostitute in the First Chorus as the Huns rush in.

It seems to me that, on the scale of transcendence, Tarakaia, whose compassion is extended to mankind, ranks higher than Kalliope, who merely reaches the point of accepting guilt. So does Hippolytus; but, in addition, his love for Phaedra is superior to the love of Tarakaia for Hermaios and of Kalliope for Demetrios. Hippolytus burns brighter than Hermaios, whose good intentions arc, after all, merely those to make a good society: he remains in the world of purpose, whereas Hippolytus and Phaedra achieve freedom in their ecstasy. Phaedra gives herself completely to the fires of creative process, but she kills herself out of fear as well as out of responsibility: her motives are mixed, impure. Nevertheless, no one surpasses her spirit except Iphigenia, whose sacrifice is absolutely pure; she goes to her death with neither guilt nor purpose, certainly not for a Greek victory. And yet we do not feel that she has tried selfishly, like Menander, to preserve her purity. Rather, she transcends the world of cause and effect, of will and purpose, even before her death.

Through love and sacrifice these characters achieve transcendence and re-create the human community. Depending on the purity of their acts, the integral person accepts varying degrees of responsibility. It is interesting that no act in the plays is specifically Christian; but the acceptance of guilt, universal compassion and love, utopianism, and pure sacrifice are essential ingredients of Christianity. The deaths of these Greeks, especially Iphigenia, foreshadow Christianity. The alternative is the blood-lust of the Huns. Rexroth has refrained from concluding with conventional Christian imagery, such as the apocalyptic passages in *Prolegomenon* and the Good Friday supper of *The Phoenix and the Tortoise*. He has learned to rely less and less on such conventions and more on *yūgen*—a hint. The acts of love and sacrifice, finally, speak for themselves. They are neither pagan nor

Christian but universal. Demetrios, Theseus, and Agamemnon still rule the world, though their names are American, Russian, French, or Chinese; and a Buddhist nun in Vietnam goes to the sacrifice as coolly as an Iphigenia.

Beyond the Mountains is, I believe, Rexroth's greatest work to date. It must be understood not merely as drama and poetry but as sacrament—and it has been performed as such by the Living Theater. As sacrament, it is a re-enactment of the mysteries of creative process, renewing our sense of identity as integral persons in community. The dilemmas are never, finally, resolved, except in death. Shall we strive for power or withdraw into the contemplative life? Is love salvation or deception? How can I be one with another, with mankind, with the universe? The answers come, not through reason or doctrine, but through involvement in such a sacrament as this, or Greek tragedy, or Japanese Nōh. The trouble is, of course, that Rexroth's is not rooted in an organic society and culture. But this terrifying condition is precisely what he is trying to overcome in all of his work. Iphigenia, Phaedra, Hippolytus show us the kind of spirit necessary for genuine community. In his next work, *The Dragon and the Unicorn,* he searches through America and Europe for the basis of such community.

II   The Dragon and the Unicorn

Rexroth tells us in the Preface to his fourth long philosophical reverie that "The form is that of the travel poems of Samuel Rogers and Arthur Hugh Clough. The general tone is not far removed from that expressed by other American travellers abroad, notably Mark Twain."[9] But there is less humor than serious quest and polemic in the poem, and Dudley Fitts has aptly observed that "It is as though in Rexroth we had a Mark Twain who had grown up; who, without yielding an iota of his sense of the absurd and the pitiful, had discarded the clown's motley for the darker dress of the comic philosopher; and who had miraculously been endowed with the power of making poetry."[10] *The Dragon and the Unicorn* (1952), is poetry of direct statement in the familiar seven-syllable line; and it resembles *The Phoenix and the Tortoise* more than the other long poems (though most of that reverie was in nine-syllable lines) as interior monologue of Rexroth's inquiry into the problem of love.

"This poem says more than it suggests," according to Richard
Eberhart. "It says a great deal. . . . This is poetic art and culture
history, with personal evaluation of a fascinating kind, managed
with freshness of insight and always some new excitement."[11]
In telling us about the world of cold war and atomic terror, the
poem reveals Rexroth's personality—the range of his concerns—
more comprehensively than any of his others. The sophisticated
traveler, the dialectical philosopher, the anarchistic polemicist,
and the lover and visionary unite in the poet as transcendent
person. And this person, universally responsible, is indispensable
for community.

The poem begins: "'And what is love?' said Pilate,/ And
washed his hands" (CLP, 95). In Part I, crossing America by
train from San Francisco to New York, and then touring England,
part of it by foot—Liverpool, Wales, Shropshire, Tintern Abbey,
Bath, Somerset, Stonehenge, London—Rexroth searches for an
answer. Some passages reminiscent of "Toward an Organic
Philosophy" and other nature poems, are lyrics of "new life" (95);
but others relate the creative process of nature to human commitment:

> All things are made new by fire.
> The plow in the furrow, Burns
> Or Buddha, the first call to
> Vocation, the severed worms,
> The shattered mouse nest, the seed
> Dripping from the bloody sword.
>   (95)

The amorality of Pilate is the kind of irresponsibility that
characterizes those who run the modern world, as men ran the
ancient one—men who deny the transforming power of love, the
universality of the human personality, and the organic nature
of the universe. Vacant lots in Chicago remind Rexroth of Andrew
Marvell's "desarts of vast eternitie" (97) and the "bombed-out
shells" of Liverpool remind him of the fall of Rome. Poverty,
war, the collapse of civilization are consequences of the amoral
use of human beings as means to an abstract, impersonal end.
They are not respected as "integral persons" but are instead
made to serve "history." The philosophical basis for such exploi-
tation is the illusion that time is "serial/ And atomic"—abstractly
objective rather than an organic dimension of human experience.

Time is made to dominate life, and extreme dehumanization is represented by "The logical positivist,/ The savage with an alarm clock," who denies the truth of any experience that cannot be verified as "scientific fact," and who, in categorically separating fact from value, denies the wholeness of organic process. Modern science, technology, and politics conspire to "quantify" the individual, making love and community more and more difficult.

The philosophical basis for renewal, according to Rexroth, lies in the recognition that "There is no reality/ Except that of experience/ And experience is the/ Conversation of persons" (106). "Conversation" is not merely verbal; it seems to mean communion, personal interaction, the sense that "all entities of/ Whatsoever nature are/ Only perspectives on persons. . ." (107). This statement is the most radical expression so far of Rexroth's personalism.

But what is a person? Not the illusion of ego, which has "no existence/ Except as the perspective/ On shifting perspectives" (112). The person seems to be the creative process itself; and he is responsible for the universe that he creates:

> Do you complain of war, famine,
> Pestilence, treason, and murder?
> They exist because you choose them.
> They are the consequences
> Of the movements of your will.
>
> (113)

Rexroth had arrived at this idea of moral responsibility at the conclusion of *The Phoenix and the Tortoise;* but here the idea is ontological: being is ethical. Reality is responsibility because a person is the universe he creates. And what is love? It is "the ultimate/ Mode of free evaluation" (121)—the act of creation itself. Rexroth's reply to Pilate is that a person is what he loves.

In Part II, Rexroth feels universal responsibility as a terrific burden. Hearing the popular song "La Vie en Rose" again and again as he travels through France, he suffers memories of failed or broken love (123-24); and, along with the pain of personal loss, he feels the agony of history—"The smoke of the Dominicans," for instance, "Frying the population" (141). Wherever he goes, he is reminded of the repression and waste of human life. How can a man of conscience find relief? Must he empathize with each individual sufferer? It appears that universal responsibility means that he must try to relate "with every person/ Who now appears as only/ One of the electrons of/ The present universe" (142)—the way of the Buddhist Boddhisattva, for example, who would renounce Buddhahood for himself in order to help humanity.

Rexroth's alternative is to seek "the transcendence/ Of the self" (141) through sexual love, which, "like all the sacraments, is a/ Miniature of being itself" (154). The union of Phaedra and Hippolytus in *Beyond the Mountains* exemplifies this kind of transcendence. The intensity of their dialogue, not to mention the passion of their dramatic act, far exceeds the feeling of *The Dragon and the Unicorn,* in which Rexroth philosophizes about love more than he presents it directly.

In Part III, as if in fulfillment of the idea of sacramental love, Rexroth tours Italy with his third wife Marthe, who conceives a child. As in previous parts, philosophizing is interspersed with anecdotal passages satirical of depersonalizing forces such as American capitalism, leftist intellectuals, the Vatican, and the state—"the/ Mechanism by which persons/ Are reduced to integers" (207). As he talks with rich intellectuals and poor workers, his thought sharpens, and the epigrams become more compressed. Love is defined as "mutual indwelling/ Without grasping" (158); it is "the final/ Form of responsibility" (156); "A person is a lover" (160). He denounces the antisexual repressiveness of the Catholic hierarchy (182) and the sexual perversions that characterize the modern commercial society in which marriage is based upon commodities (167-68). The orgiastic communion of ancient Hebrew religion—symbolized by the union of Shekinah and Jehovah—was based upon the reality of a community of lovers (173); and, in Rexroth's view, God is community (175): there is no way of knowing that He is anything else.

Community is always threatened by "collectivity"—reducing persons to numbers, as the state and the capitalist system try to do. In a world of political repression, technological coercion, and war, love is subversive: "love becomes/ As it was with the Gnostics,/ The practice of a kind of cult" (191). Lovers unite in the reality of divine community in perpetual struggle against the dehumanizing illusion of collectivity. The state is a lie; and, because people believe in it, they allow themselves to be deper-

sonalized. "Actually/ The community of lovers/ Is always there,"
for it is the universal reality of creative process. The only
alternative to despair is "to keep ourselves/ Open to the love
of others" (222).

In Part IV, while passing through Switzerland, Rexroth denounces the "spiritual masochism" of Karl Barth and the "miasma
of Jung's/ Health resort occultism" (226); then, in Paris, he
reflects on failed revolutions in the context of his anarchist
version of class struggle: "There are only two classes,/ Members
of communities,/ Members of collectivities,/ And they have
nothing in common" (230). He rejects the Marxist idea that a
collectivity such as the proletariat can usher in the good society.
"No collectivity against/ Collectivities can function/ To restore
community" (232). On the other hand, he finds community among
radical workers of sensibility and talent, who are not, however,
about to mount the barricades (236-41). Their ideology is less
important than their respect and affection for one another.
Gathering his thoughts together, he concludes that

> A community of love is
> A community of mutual
> Indwelling, in which each member
> Realizes his total
> Liability for the whole.   (241)

In the last part, back in America, traveling alone from the
East Coast to California, he stops in Chicago and Kansas City
long enough to look up a couple of girl friends and to rail at
the Protestant ethic in which "Act loses reality . . ./ A blind
plunge out of being" (253). Out West, beyond the illusions of
a civilization founded upon the denial of love, in the mountains
his thoughts travel "beyond the mountains." He sits in a cottage
in "Santa Monica Canyon where/ Andrée and I were poor and/
Happy together" (261), young artists, lovers, contemplatives:

> Far off,
> The world falls like a bomb towards
> Its own destruction. I have
> Ceased to hear it. I no longer
> Have any theories about it.
>
> . . . .
>
> Peace flows without stopping.
>   (265)

Through love, he has transcended the "empiric ego" and entered the peace of universal community.

In his introduction to the *Collected Longer Poems* he explains that "The sections in 'The Phoenix and the Tortoise' and 'The Dragon and the Unicorn' which expound a systematic view of life are dramatic dialogue, not the sole exposition of the author, and always they are contradicted by the spokesman for the other side of the polarity. If there is any dialectic resolution, it occurs each time in the unqualified transcendent experience which usually ends each long poem." On the contrary, it seems to me that much of these long poems is exposition, or internal monologue, rather than part of a dialogue; but it is true that Rexroth's dialectic, and his doctrine, are countered by direct vision in passages such as the one above.

The Dragon and the Unicorn is Rexroth's major effort to work out a philosophy of love and community. The poem suffers from the predominance of abstract thought over direct visionary experience. Nevertheless, Rexroth communicates as a man of comprehensive wisdom and deep affection. Concluding that "Perfect love casts out knowledge" (149),[12] he turned away from abstract thought in the last of the philosophical reveries in *The Collected Longer Poems: The Heart's Garden/ The Garden's Heart.* That poem, written in Japan, is almost pure vision; but more than fifteen years elapsed before it was written. In the meantime, Rexroth's reputation climbed as a leader of the San Francisco Renaissance, the expression of a new sense of community in American writing.

CHAPTER 5

Polemics and Elegies of the Atomic Age

IN THE mid-1950's Rexroth's popularity and influence rose sharply as poet, translator, critic, and mentor of the San Francisco Renaissance as well as of the Beat Generation (before he condemned it as false revolt). In 1955, limited editions were published of *A Bestiary for My Daughters Mary and Katherine* and of *Thou Shalt Not Kill: A Memorial for Dylan Thomas*— poems that were included the next year in his eighth book of original poetry, *In Defense of the Earth*. He taught at San Francisco State College, won a Chapelbrook Award and a Eunice Tietjens Award from *Poetry* magazine in 1957, and the next year received a Longview Award for *The Homestead Called Damascus*, his first philosophical reverie, which was published first in *The Quarterly Review of Literature* and then as his ninth book in 1958. He received a Shelley Memorial Award from the Poetry Society of America and an Amy Lowell Fellowship. *Bird in the Bush: Obvious Essays* and *Assays* appeared in 1959 and 1961; and six volumes of his translations of French, Japanese, Chinese, Spanish, and Greek poetry were published between 1952 and 1962. *Natural Numbers: New and Selected Poems*, the tenth book of his own poetry, appearing in 1963, provided readers with a concise overview of his poetic career.

I The San Francisco Renaissance

Rexroth's search for community began when his parents died during World War I. In Chicago's bohemia from 1918 to 1927 and in trips abroad, he became involved in the international artistic and political avant-garde, but his poetry of this period— *The Homestead Called Damascus* and *The Art of Worldly Wisdom*—indicates that he did not find what he was seeking. After moving to San Francisco in 1927, he seems to have felt a renewed sense of community, thanks to his happy marriage with

Andrée and to their proximity to ocean and mountains. Through years of Depression and World War II he struggled against the "doom of history" toward an organic philosophy. *In What Hour*, appearing in 1940, the year of Andrée's death, shows that his outlook was not yet clear; but by 1944, in *The Phoenix and the Tortoise*, he had found the basis of community in love as universal responsibility.

Undoubtedly Rexroth's sense of community continued to develop through his participation in the Bay Area avant-garde, which Professor Thomas Parkinson of Berkeley has traced back to 1944, when George Leite's *Circle* magazine first appeared with work by Rexroth, Henry Miller, Robert Duncan, Brother Antoninus, George P. Elliott, Josephine Miles and others.[1] This radical artistic community, including many who had been conscientious objectors during the war, was anarchopacifist in politics, mystical-personalist in religion, and experimental in esthetic theory and practice. Rexroth conducted in his apartment weekly seminars concerning literary, political, philosophical, and religious issues. Participants also read their poetry publicly, often with jazz accompaniment; and in 1949 they helped create the Pacifica Foundation and its first listener-sponsored radio station, KPFA-B. After a "period of dispersal" between 1950 and 1953, the opening of the Poetry Center at San Francisco State College helped revive the community. Lawrence Ferlinghetti moved to San Francisco in 1953 and established City Lights Books. Allen Ginsberg arrived in 1954, and in 1956 he read *Howl* at the famous poetry program which Kerouac describes in *The Dharma Bums* as the inauguration of the Renaissance.[2] Rexroth presided as master of ceremonies on this historic occasion; and, at the censorship trial the following year, he praised *Howl* as serious prophetic literature in the biblical tradition.[3]

In the second issue of *Evergreen Review* (1957), the New York magazine that created a mass audience for avant-garde literature, he explained the San Francisco Renaissance as a movement of cultural "disaffiliation" from the ruling "convergence of interest—the Business Community, military imperialism, political reaction, the hysterical, tear and mud drenched guilt of the ex-Stalinist, ex-Trotskyist American intellectuals, the highly organized academic and literary employment agency of the Neoantireconstructionists," and so on.[4] The polemic is grounded in the fact that the Renaissance, and the affiliated Beat movement, did

break through the widespread political cowardice and intellectual
apathy of the Dwight Eisenhower years, following the Korean
War.

In "Disengagement: the Art of the Beat Generation," an essay
in New World Writing, he traced current styles of poetry, jazz,
and action painting back through the work of two heroes of the
young who had recently died under pressure from a dehumanizing world—Dylan Thomas and Charlie Parker. "Both of them
did communicate one central theme: Against the ruin of the
world, there is only one defense—the creative act."[5] Concerning
the relation between older poets, such as Williams, Patchen, and
himself, on the one hand, and younger poets on the other—
Denise Levertov, Robert Creeley, Robert Duncan, Philip Laman-
tia, Lawrence Ferlinghetti, Allen Ginsberg, Gary Snyder, Michael
McClure, and others—"All believe in poetry as communication,
statement from one person to another. So they all avoid the
studied ambiguities and metaphysical word play of the Reactionary Generation and seek clarity of image and simplicity of
language."[6] He distinguishes sharply, however, the revolt of
serious poets and artists from "the utter nihilism of the emptied-
out hipster," and he prophesies "that most of the entire generation
will go to ruin."[7]

His distinction between creative and nihilistic revolt led him
soon to denounce the Beat Generation as "Comical bogies con-
jured up by the Luce publications."[8] You do not "nonconform,"
he wrote in "Revolt: True and False," by "caricaturing the values
of the very civilization that debauched you in the first place. . . .
The essence of revolt is understanding. . . . Literature is work.
Art is work. And work, said St. Benedict, is prayer"[9] In Rexroth's
terms, the Beats were a "public relations invention," replaced
in the 1960's by a new generation of activists who were in a
"very uncool, unbeat revolt against all the values of predatory
civilization"[10]

The civil rights, antiwar, student-power and black-power activists impress Rexroth as a more responsible generation than the
Beats; but he does not deny the genuine poetic accomplishments
of Ginsberg, of Ferlinghetti, and especially of Snyder. The
controversy is confused because such poets as Denise Levertov
and Robert Duncan are often falsely included in the Beat movement, whereas Rexroth never meant to include them in his attack.
His old friend Lawrence Lipton has recently tried to revive the

controversy. "When the Beat writers began to steal the spotlight in press and media," Lipton wrote, Rexroth "went into a sulk from which he never emerged. . . ."[11] On the contrary, he has been an exceptionally active and influential poet, translator, and essayist from the mid-1950's to the present.

II In Defense of the Earth *and Translations*

Rexroth's book of the Beat period, *In Defense of the Earth,* (1956), is no period piece. After a decade and a half, these poems of love and protest, of meditation and remembrance, stand out as some of his most deeply felt poems. Though many are about his life in San Francisco—watching stars above "the Christmas Eve crowds/ On Fillmore Street, the Negro/ District," for instance,[12] or hiking among redwoods, or in the mountains with his daughter, as in "Mary and the Seasons"—there is little topicality that links them to the Beat movement. Moreover, the themes are those that have always preoccupied him, and the style of most of them is, in R. W. Flint's words, "plain statement and lyric celebration, secure in old lives, affections, achievements, and memories."[13] Muriel Rukeyser has praised the poet for "a lyric-mindedness" and "a learning that eats the gifts of the world."[14] In *The Modern Poets,* M. L. Rosenthal praised "The Mirror in the Woods" (CSP, 257), "Blood on a Dead World" (242), and "Our Home Is in the Rocks" (253) for their " 'savage' relation to truth"; and, though he criticized "Thou Shalt Not Kill: A Memorial for Dylan Thomas" (267-75) for "the self-indulgent pleasure of the poet in love with his own oratory," he nevertheless called him "the strongest of these West Coast anarchist poets because he is a good deal more than a West Coast anarchist poet. He is a man of wide cultivation,"[15] as we know.

Because "Thou Shalt Not Kill" has often been mocked as if Rexroth's reputation as a poet essentially depended on it, it should be discussed before the love poems with which the book begins. The elegy for Thomas—and for all poet-seers—begins:

> They are murdering all the young men.
> For half a century now, every day,
> They have hunted them down and killed them.
> (267)

Rosenthal admits that these lines are "a magnificently passionate beginning whose power carries over to, and is taken up by, the later *ubi sunt* stanzas which call the roll of the modern poets who have died, sickened, given up, been imprisoned, or gone mad. . ."(166).

> What happened to Robinson,
> Who used to stagger down Eighth Street,
> Dizzy with solitary gin?
> Where is Masters, who crouched in
> His law office for ruinous decades?
> Where is Leonard who thought he was
> A locomotive? And Lindsay,
> Wise as a dove, innocent
> As a serpent, where is he?
> Timor mortis conturbat me.

(169)

Protest has turned into an elegy of bewilderment which is fully as tender as the sixteenth-century "Lament for the Makeris" by the Scottish poet William Dunbar, from which Rexroth derived the form and refrain. Death, Dunbar wrote,

> hes done petuously devour
> The noble Chaucer, of makaris flowr,
> The Monk of Bery, and Gower, all thre:
> *Timor mortis conturbat me.*[16]

Tenderness, however, does not obscure the horror of poets' deaths, as Rexroth catalogues them: Hart Crane's suicide and the murder of Maxwell Bodenheim, for instance.

> All over the world
> The same disembodied hand
> Strikes us down.
> Here is a mountain of death.
> A hill of heads like the Khans piled up.
> The first-born of a century
> Slaughtered by Herod.
> Three generations of infants
> Stuffed down the maw of Moloch.

(272)

In the last part of the poem, as he turns to Dylan Thomas, the prophetic style becomes lyrical:

> He is dead.
> The bird of Rhiannon.
> He is dead.
> In the winter of the heart.
> (272)

Suddenly, accusation breaks through the lyricism: "You drowned him in your cocktail brain./ He fell down and died in your synthetic heart" (273). It is this concluding section that offends many readers who are sensitive, perhaps, to the point of being self-righteous. The natural response is to recoil: How am *I* responsible? Rexroth accuses "Oppenheimer the Million-killer," "Einstein the Grey Eminence," Hemingway, Eliot, and many others (273); but always the finger of guilt returns to the reader. Why?

Rexroth seems to be saying that anyone who thrives, or even survives, in an antipersonal culture has climbed on the "mountain of death." The successful have helped create, or at least sustain, a culture that destroys the young and talented, if not in war then in the acquisitive society at home. But if that is true generally, surely not everyone is *personally* responsible for Thomas' death. What about readers who do not wear Brooks Brothers suits? What about Rexroth himself? It is true that he does not seem to feel personally responsible; in desperation he considers terrorism: "I want to run into the street,/ Shouting, 'Remember Vanzetti!'/ I want to pour gasoline down your chimneys" (274). As a successful poet, does he take any of the guilt? Certainly his assumption of total moral liability—expressed in *The Phoenix and the Tortoise, Beyond the Mountains,* and *The Dragon and the Unicorn*—would lead to the insight that much of his rage and indignation are explosions from his own involvement in the very culture that he denounces. While he curses the culture, his poem becomes a part of it. Perhaps he is self-righteous, but he has unforgettably exposed the "social lie" that has destroyed dozens of poets.

"Thou Shalt Not Kill" is Rexroth's best protest poem, I believe, because of its range of feeling from tenderness to bewilderment, thence to prophetic rage and accusation. Though W. C. Williams had reservations about some of the other poems in the volume, he was enthusiastic about this one: "It should be posted in the clubrooms of all universities so that it could never be forgotten."[17] Read with jazz accompaniment, the poem, as prophetic assault and public sacrament of mourning, is unforgettable.

But of course many poems in the book are meditative, "seeking

over and over again," as he states in the Preface, "for the changing forms of an unchanging significance in stars, insects, mountains and daughters. They do not of course try to answer, 'Why
am I here?' 'Why is it out there?'—but to snare the fact that is
the only answer, the only meaning of present or presence" (7).
Sadly, an important fact has been obscured in *The Collected
Shorter Poems*: the central importance of his wife Marthe in the
1956 volume. It was dedicated to her, the first seven poems were
a sequence for her, and the next poem was titled "The Great
Canzon for Marthe." The book was essentially a celebration of
marriage and their family: poems for her were followed by poems
for their children, Mary (born 1950) and Katherine (born 1954)
—the sequences called "The Lights in the Sky Are Stars," "Mary
and the Seasons," "A Bestiary," and "Mother Goose," as well as
individual poems to them. But following the divorce in 1961,
Marthe's name was omitted from *The Collected Shorter Poems*,
and the poems were rearranged. Much of the unity and beauty
of the book have been sacrificed in what must have been a heart-
breaking experience.

But the love poems, almost unbearably poignant, remain true
to the "unchanging significance" of "the wonderful,/ Unending,
unfathomable/ Process of becoming each/ Ourselves for each
other" (233). For instance, watching her sleeping face,

> I knew then,
> As your secret spoke, my secret self,
> The blind bird, hardly visible in
> An endless web of lies. And I knew
> The web too, its every knot and strand,
> The hidden crippled bird, the terrible web.
>   (228)

Self-discovery is also the theme of a number of poems about
his own youth—the one beginning, "In my childhood when I
first" (227); "A Living Pearl" (234), about his trip west at age
sixteen; "For Eli Jacobson" (224), about the good days of being
hopeful young revolutionists together, and "The Bad Old Days"
(258) in the Chicago stockyards district in 1918 when he took
a vow of revolution. But, as in his earlier poems, the deepest
discovery of self occurs in moments when the self is transcended
in vision or love:

> Blood flows out to the fleeing
> Nebulae, and flows back, red

> With all the worn space of space,
> Old with all the time of time.
> It is my blood. I cannot
> Taste in it as it leaves me
> More of myself than on its
> Return. I can see in it
> Trees of silence and fire.
> I can see faces. Mostly
> They are your face.
>
> (227)

In "Time Is the Mercy of Eternity" he develops the theme that "The holiness of the real is always there, accessible/ In total immanence" (248), a metaphysic manifested in his translations of Japanese poems near the end of the book. They are followed by a pair of poems called "They Say This Isn't a Poem." The first presents an impersonal metaphysic—"All that is is a harmony,/ Otherwise it would not endure"—which is "beautiful and specious/ ... stinking with the blood/ Of wars and crucifixions." The second poem develops the wiser view that "The order of the universe/ Is only a reflection/ Of the human will and reason" (312-13). Finally, "Codicil" tells us that poetry which is supposed to be "impersonal construction"—by Eliot, Valéry, and Pope, for instance—turns out to be

> intense,
> Subjective revery as
> Intimate and revealing,
> Embarrassing if you will,
> As the indiscretions of
> The psychoanalyst's couch.
> There is always sufficient
> Reason for the horror of
> The use of the pronoun, "I."
>
> (314)

For the self, responsible for all it experiences and creates, is ultimately indistinguishable from its universe. From beginning to end the book explores the universe as a community in which Rexroth's childhood, marriage, children, and friends are central. He is less philosophical than in *The Phoenix and the Tortoise,* less concerned with abstract thought, because in these poems community has been realized. It is not a theory but a fact.

Rexroth's style of lyrical direct statement, as well as his organic

vision of nature, seems to have been shaped, ever since his discovery of Tu Fu in adolescence, through his translations of
Oriental poetry, such as the forty-five Japanese poems in this
volume. The first is perhaps typical:

> All day I hoe weeds.
> All night I sleep.
> All night I hoe again
> In dreams the weeds of the day.
> *Anonymous* (299)

Others appear in *One Hundred Poems from the Japanese* (1955).
Concerning the companion volume, *One Hundred Poems from
the Chinese* (1956), W. C. Williams called it "one of the most
brilliantly sensitive books of poems in the American idiom it has
ever been my good fortune to read.... As a translator of the
Chinese lyrics of Tu Fu, his ear is finer than anyone I have ever
encountered."[18]

It would take a critic as erudite and as sensitive as Rexroth to
evaluate his full accomplishments as a translator, but there is no
question about his facility with the American idiom, which is
more convincing, I think, than Pound's mannerisms. Other books
of Rexroth's translations are *Fourteen Poems by O. V. de L.
Milosz* (1952), *One Hundred French Poems* (1955), *Thirty
Spanish Poems of Love and Exile* (1956), *Poems from the Greek
Anthology* (1962), *Selected Poems of Pierre Reverdy* (1969),
and *Love in the Turning Year: One Hundred More Poems from
the Chinese* (1970).

III *Essays*

Most of Rexroth's essays of the 1950's were collected in *Bird
in the Bush: Obvious Essays* (1959) and *Assays* (1961), but the
ones about the Beats were saved for *The Alternative Society*
(1970). Of the collected essays, he insists in his introduction to
the first volume that "These pieces are not criticism but journal-
ism" in "the tradition of Huneker, Mencken, Wilson" (vi).
Most were written on assignment, all for pay, and none for
academic quarterlies. But they are marked by erudition and
subtlety of thought and feeling as well as by humor and polemical
brilliance. Alfred Kazin, reviewing them, called Rexroth a dil-
ettante and an "old-fashioned American sorehead of the type of

the Populists screaming against the moneyed east"[19]; but Richard Foster, a latter-day New Critic and a self-admitted "standard academic," surprisingly found much to praise. *Bird in the Bush,* he wrote, "read like a good novel—subtle, vivid, intense, and deeply compelling. And cumulatively it created, as both good essay and good fiction creates, character: a person who moves, speaks, lives in its pages—Rexroth."[20] The epigrammatical and polemical style, he explained, gives us "a sense of voice, the continuity and integrity of the person as an authentic moral identity."

Foster cites some of his favorite epigrams from Rexroth, such as, "The greater poetry is nobly disheveled. It never shows the scars of taking care," and "True humor is the most effective mode of courage."[21] Some of mine are: "No truck with the Social Lie" (BB, viii); "Genuine revolt goes with an all-too-definite life aim— hardly with the lack of it" (43); "The stuff of life, of art, is not only vaster far than all programs and careers, it is the material of a different qualitative world altogether" (64); "'When a prophet refuses to go crazy, he becomes quite a problem, crucifixion being as complicated as it is in humanitarian America" (76-77); and "Heroism is only smouldering and will flame up after these dark ages are over" (84). These judgments resound with wisdom, both as isolated epigrams and in the context of the essays.

Erudite as Aristotle but colloquial as Socrates, dialectical as Marx but as funny as Mark Twain, Rexroth is full of surprises. He slides an idiosyncratic insight into a subordinate clause as if it were an afterthought, or he summarizes centuries of Chinese or Jewish thought as if it were as familiar as the story of his own life. In fact, it *is* the story of his own life. Unlike scholars who keep their distance from objectively framed subjects, he has absorbed and tested whatever he has studied, trying it out not only intellectually but also emotionally, imaginatively, and often practicably—meditating like Lao Tzu or painting like Sesshu, for instance.[22] Thomas Parkinson has commented on his "trick of imaginative projections that allowed him to suggest he was a contemporary of Lenin, Whitman, Tu Fu, Thoreau, Catullus, Baudelaire, John Stuart Mill—they were all so real to him."[23] To paraphrase W. C. Williams' slogan, "No ideas but in things," Rexroth's sense of life, in the essays as in the poetry, seems to be, "No ideas but in persons; no ideas but in I-Thou."

In discussing Rexroth's philosophy of the "irreducible man,"

Foster compares him to "St. Francis for simplicity, Buddha for purity, Martin Buber for joy and good will, Sacco and Vanzetti for everyday conscience and courage, and Lawrence for passion and intelligence."[24] But it is not enough to imagine Rexroth as a synthesis of their qualities; he is more than that because he is a unique sensibility, just as each of the others is too unique and complex to be reduced to a few qualities or ideas. The Person is a mystery; and, despite Rexroth's brilliant powers of definition, analysis, and judgment, he embodies the mystery of creative personality that lies beyond the range of ideas. "Everybody has a lot of fakery in his make-up" (viii), Rexroth writes, recognizing his own fallibility, providing comic relief for his more grandiose utterances, and revealing himself as a unique mystery who somehow communicates with other mysteries.

The mystery of human personality is best expressed, perhaps, through humor, irony, paradox; through sudden shifts in tone; through extremes of diction—all qualities of Rexroth's style. Foster comments on "comic incongruity as a counterpoint to the principle of tragic awareness" (135), which Rexroth calls "Homeric" humor in his essay on American humor. It seems to me that it might just as well be called "Jewish humor" or "Zen humor" or the humor of Samuel Beckett or Mark Twain—and Rexroth displays it when writing on these and other subjects. This sense of humor saves him from pomposity and system-building, to which he is inclined by virtue of his intellectual vigor. Ideas accepted absolutely are a joke on the human race. Religions and philosophies turn out to be, at best, beautiful creations of the imagination—seductive but highly fallible.

Rexroth has never written a comprehensive prose exposition of his philosophy because, as the mathematician Gödel proved, "a self-contained system is a contradiction of terms" (quoted on the title page of *Gödel's Proof: New Poems*, 1965, CSP, 1). In his poems, he is in dialogue with himself, never finally certain of his ideas; and, in his essays, his ideas emerge through confrontation with artists, thinkers, and poets such as Martin Buber, D. H. Lawrence, Samuel Beckett, and Chinese sages. Insight flares from this confrontation, as in his critique of Buber's belief in God:

> As a poem, *I and Thou* is very beautiful. But it is this metaphysical greed which removes it from the category of the highest art. There is amongst men no absolute need. The realization of this

is what makes Homer and the Greek tragedians so much sounder a Bible than the Old or New testaments. Love does not last forever, friends betray each other, beauty fades, the mighty stumble in blood and their cities burn. The ultimate values are love and friendship and courage and magnanimity and grace, but it is a narrow ultimate, and lasts only a little while, contingent on the instability of men and the whims of "Nature viewed as a Thou." Like life, it is Helen's tragedy that gives her her beauty or gives Achilles and Agamemnon their nobility. Any art which has a happy ending in reserve in Infinity is, just to that degree, cheating. (139)

In this passage, and in many others throughout *Bird in the Bush*, Rexroth suggests the moral range of his thinking without binding it into a system. His Personalism is esthetic, for man is a creative being; art, therefore, reveals as much of the mystery of human existence as we can know. In "Unacknowledged Legislators and *Art pour Art*" (3-18), the most comprehensive statement of his esthetics, he discusses poetry as the communication of sensibility. Poetry "increases and guides our awareness to immediate experience and to the generalizations which can be made from immediate experience" (6). Personal awareness becomes generalized into ethical and cultural norms: "As acuteness grows and becomes more organized in the individual and in society as a whole—in the separate individuals who make up the abstraction 'society as a whole'—it reorganizes and restates the general value judgments of the society. We become more clearly aware of what is good and bad, interesting and dull, beautiful and ugly, lovable and mean" (6). Poetry is fundamentally communication, but "Purposive construction of any kind is a species of communication" (7). Both Jackson Pollack's "art of random occasion" and Eliot's supposedly impersonal "objective correlatives" communicate the individual sensibilities of the artists (7 and 8).

In communicating, "the arts do not differ in kind from ordinary speech"—though they communicate more, and more deeply. There is, however, no separate "realm" of art distinct from life (9). And, in fact, "you can apprehend even the simplest speech or simplest plastic arrangement . . . with the intensity of an artistic experience. . . . It is the attention that creates the structure" (10). Communication becomes a problem only because "people become more like things than persons to each other"—what Buber called the "I-It" relation and what Marx regarded as "reification," the transformation of sensuous experience into oppressive abstractions, such as "profit" and "capital."[25] The process, according to Rexroth, is as follows: "First, alienation from comradeship in the struggle with nature, then alienation from each other, finally self-alienation" (12).

Poetry reverses the process, communicating "self to self—whole 'universes of discourse' " (12) and changing the sensibility, which "deepens, widens, becomes more intense and complex, in the interchange between person and person" (13). Of course, poets are not always fully aware of what they communicate, especially if they are programmatic: for instance, Baudelaire, Blake, Auden— and one might add Rexroth himself. "However," he tells us, "there are rare instances where the 'message,' the expository occasion that floats as it were the poetic accomplishment, is itself so profound, so deep an utterance of a fully realized person that it augments the poetry and raises it to the highest level," as in Homer and in the great Chinese poets (17-18). It goes without saying that this kind of philosophical poetry is what Rexroth himself has been engaged in writing.

In other essays he develops his theory of poetry as personal vision, as interpersonal communication, and as communal sacrament. In a discussion of jazz, for example, he shows how organic rhythms of speech, song, music, and dance unite men in communities (19-42). And implications for the visual arts are discussed in essays on J. M. W. Turner (204), Mark Tobey (16), Fernand Léger (224), and most effectively, I think, in "The Visionary Painting of Morris Graves," in which we are told that the function of the artist is the revelation of reality in process, of permanence in change, of the place of value in a world of facts. "His duty is to keep open the channels of contemplation and to discover new ones. His role is purely revelatory" (57).

Assays (1961) is a less impressive book, but some fine essays extend the idea of *Bird in the Bush*. In "The Poet as Translator," for instance, Rexroth illustrates "Dryden's main thesis—that the translation of poetry into poetry is an act of sympathy—the identification of another person with oneself, the transference of his utterance to one's own utterance" (19). And in "American Indian Songs" he emphasizes "the crucial importance of song, and hence of the work of art, as the very link of significant life itself, of the individual to his society, of the individual to his human and nonhuman environment" (57). "Sung Culture" (1-13) and "Science and Civilization in China" (82-86), moreover, should be read along with 'The Chinese Classic Novel in Translation" (in *Bird in the Bush*, 213-23) for background to Rexroth's oriental poems and Buddhist consciousness.

"The Holy Kabbalah" (*Assays*, 441-51) and "Gnosticism" (131-42) develop the theme of "The Hasidism of Martin Buber" (in *Bird in the Bush*, (106-42), the idea of "I-Thou" that is crucial for an understanding of Rexroth's Personalism. "The Influence of French Poetry on American" is one of the most informative of all his "assays" (143-74). And others about W. C. Williams and the new poetry of the 1950's and about Lawrence Durrell, Henry James, H. G. Wells, Mark Twain, and others should be considered along with essays about such writers as Kenneth Patchen, Samuel Beckett, Henry Miller, D. H. Lawrence, W. B. Yeats, Arthur Rimbaud, and Charles Baudelaire in *Bird in the Bush*.

Richard Foster raised some objections to *Assays*, despite his admiration for "The Influence of French Poetry on American" and other essays. He was particularly incensed by "a mad essay called 'The Students Take Over' which announces a nationwide revolution among students on behalf of national and international integrity"[26]—a prediction that has turned out to be fairly accurate. Foster also objected to Rexroth's favoring Mark Twain over Henry James and to his lack of Alfred Kazin's "deep, deep seriousness"—whatever that means. But Foster concluded that Rexroth is an "original" who is "splendidly vital and intelligent."[27] A reader of Foster's critique may feel that the academic critic, ashamed of his earlier enthusiasm for Rexroth, wrote a review of the second collection as a kind of penance.

Unfortunately, the second review reveals less of Foster's humanism than the first, in which he had seemed to be on the edge of fresh discoveries. "Rexroth is articulating," he had written, "—and with a significant shade more of personal commitment, I feel—the same philosophy of humane letters that has been expounded over the past thirty years by Eliot, Richards, Tate, Blackmur, and the majority of our most influential and respected critics."[28] This was high praise for an anarchist who called academic poets "corn-belt metaphysicals," and it appears that Foster was trying to "eat crow" in his second review. He certainly did not try to reconcile Rexroth with Eliot and the New Criticism, but perhaps it can be done.

The context for such a reconciliation would have to be the humanistic tradition not only of the West but also of Asia. Rexroth's third book of essays, *Classics Revisited* (1968), must convincingly demonstrate even to the most skeptical and exclusive academic that Rexroth is at home in this tradition. These essays, which originally appeared in *Saturday Review*, are less polemical and more patient than those in *Bird in the Bush* and in *Assays*. His remarks about sixty classics, ranging from Greek epics to *Huckleberry Finn* and Chekhov's plays, show that he has absorbed the wisdom of many literatures. In the first essay, on the Sumerian *Epic of Gilgamesh*, he touches on some of the universal themes that author after author, including himself, has explored, each from a unique perspective:

The absurdity of life and death, heroic wistfulness, nostalgia for lost possibilities, melancholy of missed perfection were as meaningful five thousand years ago to the Sumerians as they are to us. We look at them today in museum cases—round heads, curly hair, immense eyes and noses, plump hands folded over plump chests, cloaks like leaves or feathers—and they look out at us, and we know that they knew that the love of comrades cannot prevail against the insult of death, that erotic women destroy men with impossible demands, that nothing endures, that the memory of heroic action lasts a little while and sometimes the walls of empire a little longer, that the meaning of life can be revealed but never explained, and that the realization of these truths constitutes the achievement of true personality. (7)

IV   Natural Numbers

In 1956 New Directions published *The Homestead Called Damascus*, written three decades earlier, and in 1963 *Natural Numbers: New and Selected Poems*, his tenth book of original poetry, which is about one-third the size of *The Collected Shorter Poems* (342 pages). Few of the early poems are included in *Natural Numbers*—less than a dozen pages from his first two books. Notably missing are rhetorical poems of revolutionary hope and despair, of intricate philosophizing, and of the stylistic extremes of his Cubist experiments—although a gentle Cubism is apparent in "A Lesson in Geography," from *In What Hour* and in "Eight for Ornette's Music" among the "New Poems (1957-1962)":

> if the pain is greater
> than the difference
> as the bird in the night
> or the perfumes in the moon
> oh witch of question
> oh lips of submission
> in the flesh of summer
> the silver slipper
> in the sleeping forest
> (CSP, 332)

These poems for jazz accompaniment, and "This Night Only," written for Eric Satie's music (CSP, 338), are among the most erotic and are stylistically the most experimental. Nearly all of the other "New Poems" are in Rexroth's more conventional, direct statement in syllabics, and the prevailing tone is deeply elegiac rather than lyrical or satirical.

In many of the "New Poems" he is hiking and fishing with his daughters; listening to Mary, at seven, talk wisely about "Homer in Basic" (317); reminiscing about "the years/ Of revolutionary/ Hope" ("Fish Peddler and Cobbler," 319); or remembering his father flipping poker chips as three-year-old Katherine plays with some old ones. A dozen poems written during travels in France, Italy, and England are very like passages in *The Dragon and the Unicorn*, but we find none of the harshness of his earlier satire; for he has moved from polemical protest to tragic acceptance of the human condition. In "May Day," for instance:

> They are pushing all this pretty
> Planet, Venice, and Palladio,
> And you and me, and the golden
> Sun, nearer and nearer to
> Total death. Nothing can stop them.
> (330-31)

The book ends with a sequence called "Air and Angels," love poems with the insistent, sad reminder of inevitable loss and loneliness, as in Matthew Arnold's "Dover Beach," from which Rexroth quotes in "Pacific Beach" (340-41). No philosophizing can save him from the overriding sense of doom surrounding moments of passionate vision. Generally, I think that the "New Poems" as a unit is less impressive than *In Defense of the Earth* or *The Signature of All Things*, though "Fish Peddler and Cobbler" (318) is one of his best reminiscences of the "years of revolutionary hope," and the poems written in Aix-en-Provence and in Venice (321-31) are not inferior, stylistically, to *The Dragon and the Unicorn*.

What is missing from the "New Poems" is the philosophical and stylistic range, the extremes of thought and feeling, that made *The Dragon and the Unicorn* such an exciting book. In the "New Poems" he is doing what he has already done so well, but without the grand conception, the polemical thrust, the "turn" of attitude that characterized each of his previous books. Moreover, in selecting from his earlier work, he has omitted from *Natural Numbers* such revolutionary utterances as "August 22, 1939" and "Thou Shalt Not Kill," as well as nearly all of his Cubist experiments. The quieter, more traditional side of his personality emerges in this book. He seems to be consolidating his life-work, in resignation, in a mood of "lonely, empty, tenderness" (339).

Of course, resignation has been an underlying mood in his work ever since he wrote *Homestead*. *In What Hour* shows how his revolutionary hopes rose and fell during the 1930's, and the angry passages of *The Phoenix and the Tortoise, The Dragon and the Unicorn,* and "Thou Shalt Not Kill" derive from a sense that the world will not improve, that history is a kind of fate. His rage and vision are heroic responses to the inevitability of death, to the collapse of community, and to the end of the human race. His sense of life is as tragic as is that of Homer or Sophocles.

Several events deepened his disillusionment and resignation. First, his divorce from Marthe in 1961 ended the celebration of matrimonial love on which his "anthropological religion" rested and out of which he had written some of his finest love poems as well as his playful sequences to their daughters, Mary and Katherine ("A Bestiary" and "Mother Goose"). Second, the cold war and the threat of nuclear annihilation persisted. World leaders precipitated crisis after crisis—Suez, Cuba, Vietnam. "They are killing the young men," he had written in his memorial for Dylan Thomas (267), and nothing can stop them. Third, the Beat Generation, far from undermining the culture of death through "disaffiliation" and the creation of genuine community, had become, in his view, a comedy act for the mass media.

Perhaps Rexroth's own fame also contributed to his resignation. During the 1950's he became an international celebrity, hated by many established poets and critics; loved by younger, more independent writers and intellectuals; and admired as much as he was feared. His poetry, his criticism, and his encouragement of poets such as Denise Levertov and Gary Snyder, as well as his central role in the San Francisco Renaissance, helped change the course of American poetry, liberating it from the academic strictures of the New Criticism. His example and influence have helped make American poetry more honest and direct, emotionally richer, more genuinely visionary. His translations have helped acquaint many young poets with Chinese and Japanese poetry, and his essays on Oriental art and thought have contributed to our understanding of Taoism and Buddhism. People from all over the world regard Rexroth as a guru, visiting him for knowledge and advice.

And yet, like Socrates, he asks himself in poem after poem, "What do I know?" Since *The Dragon and the Unicorn* he has published no long poems, and few short ones, in which the dialectic of abstract ideas plays a central role. He seems less interested in the major issues of Western philosophy and more in the perfection of direct sensuous vision. Everything else, including his own fame, is an illusion. Though he has always been a visionary, he spent more than three decades searching for a philosophical rationale for his experience, for history, and for nature. In the 1960's he seems to have abandoned that kind of quest in favor of pure visionary experience. His fifth long poem, *The Heart's Garden/ The Garden's Heart* (1968), an extended Buddhist-Taoist meditation written in Japan, shows the depths of his resignation and enlightenment.

CHAPTER 6

"The Climax of the Rite of Rebirth"

NEW Directions published *The Collected Shorter Poems*—
Rexroth's eleventh book of original poetry—in 1966, the
same year that Doubleday issued *An Autobiographical Novel.*
Meanwhile, in 1964, Rexroth had taught at San Francisco State
College and, in the summer, at the University of Wisconsin—
Milwaukee, as writer-in-residence. He had received a grant from
the National Academy of Arts and Letters that same year and,
the next, the William Carlos Williams Award from *Contact*
magazine. In 1967 he traveled around the world on a grant from
the Rockefeller Foundation, for the purpose of visiting European
and Asian cultural centers and an Akademische Austauschdienst
Award made it possible for him to live in West Germany for
several months. *The Heart's Garden / The Garden's Heart*—
his twelfth book of poetry—appeared also in 1967, and *The Collected Longer Poems* the next, climaxing his career so far.

I   The Collected Shorter Poems

The Collected Shorter Poems (1966) begins with a section of
new poems called "Gödel's Proof," after which the poems are
arranged book by book from *The Art of Worldly Wisdom* (1920-
30) through *Natural Numbers* (1964), more or less in the order
in which they were written. On the title page, the quotation from
the mathematician Gödel—"A self-contained system is a contradiction of terms. QED"—expresses Rexroth's withdrawal from
his efforts to construct a comprehensive philosophy in his long
poems. Since adolescence, he had known that no system could
cover all human contingencies; nevertheless, he had heroically
tried to explain the mysteries of human existence, his efforts
being checked by skepticism on the one hand and transcended
in visionary experience on the other. The new poems are devoid

of the dialectic and satire of *The Dragon and the Unicorn,* but the sensuousness and the anguish have deepened.

At the beginning of "Gödel's Proof," in the sequence of four poems called "Andromeda Chained to Her Rock the Great Nebula in Her Heart" (3-5), Rexroth seems to be returning to the dissociation and despair of his earliest work. Throughout this sequence, the ache and the fear are unrelieved. The only hint of transcendence is in "The bite of the gods/ In the wilderness" (5). This sequence is the most emotionally intense of his Cubist poems, perhaps because the abstract ideas do not contain the language and feeling, as they did in "Prolegomenon to a Theodicy."

Out of this despair, Rexroth celebrates the momentary joys of love in "Travelers in Erewhon" (6), "Time is an Inclusion Series Said McTaggart" (12), and other poignant poems of direct statement. Again, these poems are reminiscent of his early work; one, in fact, about a pickup named Nada, is entitled "Oaxaca 1925" (7). These poems read as if he is swinging through the cycle of despair, love, separation, and loneliness again; but doing so this time without the comforts of philosophizing. The mysteries of love are evoked with no explanation, no argument. Often, the lovers seem to be wrapped in light or heat or snow or water: "in the smoky light of the old/ Oil lamp your shoulders/ Belly breasts buttocks/ Are all like peach blossoms/ . . . In the black world/ In the country of eyes" (6). Or they wander "Through a sweltering summer/ Of guitars and gunfire and tropical leaves/ And black shadows in the moonlight . . ."(7). Or "You beside me/ Like a colt swimming slowly in kelp/ In the nude sea . . ." (10).

There is a hint of transcendence in a brief Christmas poem called "Phaedo" (13), but a couple of Cubist poems (14, 16) in which he is more playful cut into the more serious mood. This mood is re-established, however, in several poems about his family—"A Flute Overhead" (19), "The Wheel Revolves" (20), "Organization Men in Affluent Society" (21), and "The Hanged Man" (22)—and we begin to feel that he has emerged, again, from despair through erotic Duality into the "ethical mysticism of sacramental marriage" (as he put it in his introduction to *The Phoenix and the Tortoise,* p. 8). But suddenly, in the last of these poems, he strikes a note of terrible disillusionment—

the "Realization that love assumed and trusted/ Through years
of mutual life/ Had never been there at all" (22).

Uncertain of love, what can he depend upon? What remains
after marriage fails? Only the cycles of nature—the "Yin and
Yang," the title of his last original poem in "Gödel's Proof" (before
three Chinese translations that complete this section of *The Collected Shorter Poems*). Of all Rexroth's nature poems, this one
is the most liturgical:

> The flowers are back in their places.
> The birds back in their usual trees.
> The winter stars set in the ocean.
> The summer stars rise from the mountains.
> The air is filled with atoms of quicksilver.
> Resurrection envelops the earth.
>
> (23)

The language is direct and simple; the archetypes come effort-
lessly, in harmonious balance with one another, in syntactic
parallels. The astrological descriptions are really not obscure.
Moving from Leo into Virgo, the moon fertilizes her, and the
"glittering wheat ear" has symbolized the processes of creation
ever since the Eleusinian mysteries. This "climax," having "ascend-
ed from the underworld" as the constellations turn in the evening,
is "proclaimed" in moonlight, while under the world the "sun
swims" in Pisces, the double fish and the Chinese symbol of Yin
and Yang, dark/light, cold/heat, female/male, and so on. The
poem is itself cyclic, from the sun at the end to the moon at
the beginning.

The prosody is also impressive, the basic pattern being syllabic.
All but three lines have nine syllables. The eleven syllables of
"The air is filled with atoms of quicksilver" quicken the pace;
and the last two lines, having eight syllables each, are slower,
and more gnomic, than the others: "In the underworld the sun
swims/ Between the fish called Yes and No." Emerging from
the syllabic movement, however, is a triple accentual pattern
in the lines about flowers, birds, winter, and summer stars, the
most emphatic being "The líon gives the móon to the Vírgin./
She stánds at the cróssroads of héaven." There is a definite
dactyllic movement in many lines which never becomes mechanical, firmly supporting the prophetic tone.

Concerning his prosody in general, Rexroth has written that

against the syllabic count "is counterpointed a rhythm primarily of quantity, secondarily of accent. In addition, close attention is paid to the melodic line of the vowels and to the evolution of consonents (p-b-k, m-r-l-y, *etc.*)."[1] In "Yin and Yang," for example, the "melodic line" begins with short *i*'s, but opens up into *o*'s, *a*'s, and *u*'s; and they go through subtle variations: from *spring* to *range*, from *warm* to *perfumed*, from *under* to *Easter moon*, on an underlying stream of sibilants.

In an excellent discussion of Rexroth's prosody, Lawrence Lipton has explained the syllabic line as Rexroth's means of breaking "the sound barrier of English verse"—the iambic beat. "Nothing breaks the habit of iambic better than the discipline of practicing to breathe, so to speak, in seven syllable intervals. Or nine syllables. Eight, if you must, but never ten. Well, hardly ever"; and Lipton observes that Rexroth's syllabics are flexible, for he is "no word-chopper with a box of hyphens in his tool chest. . . . Rexroth justifies his practice in the only way any metric can be justified, by making vocally viable verse with it. Perhaps, like William Carlos Williams, he tends to think of iambic as English rather than American prosody."[2]

But could not much of Rexroth's material, especially the philosophical passages, be presented as poetic prose? Lipton makes an astute reply: "It could, without losing its sense or its tone, but it would lose the pace which the poet wishes to give his words. After all, that is what line-length is for: a formal notation of the poet's tempo, the pace and emphasis he prescribes for the oral rendition of the verse. There is more opportunity here for alternating legato with staccato passages than the longer, flowing line of poetic prose permits."[3] It seems to me that changes of pace are particularly effective in "Yin and Yang," beginning as it does with the stately and languid "It is spring once more in the Coast Range/ Warm, perfumed, under the Easter moon," then quickening with the sharp accents of the next lines of emphatic parallelism, but slowing down in the last two lines of the poem.

Besides "Yin and Yang" only one other of the new poems is in regular syllabic lines—"Organization Men in Affluent Society" (21). "Song for a Dancer" (his daughter Mary) is in ballad stanzas. The other poems are in rhythms that are much freer than those that characterize most of his poetry, as if, in returning to the bewilderment of immediate sensuous experience, he has

had to abandon prosodic along with philosophical preconceptions.
Sometimes there are jazz cadences as in "Travelers in Erewhon":

> You open your
> Dress on the dusty
> Bed where no one
> Has slept for years
> An owl moans on the roof
> (6)

And the freer rhythms generally make Rexroth seem less intellectual, more spontaneous, uncertain, even reckless, than in most
of his work. He seems to have aged through wisdom into a kind
of second youth, in which each mortal instant is lived fully.

The anguish and tenderness of the new poems are intensified
by the feeling that no instant of life can be redeemed. All passes
away. Flowers, birds, stars return, as in "Yin and Yang"; but
they are not the same. Even if patterns are eternal, the particulars
of experience are not. In "The Wheel Revolves," Rexroth's daughter is like a reincarnation of the dancer in a poem by Po Chu I;
and, as summer and swallows return, "Ten thousand years
revolve without change./ All this will never be again" (21).
Faith in the eternal process of creation cannot save the particular
day, or daughter, from mutability.

Turning from the new poems to some of his earliest in *The Art
of Worldly Wisdom*, one is struck, after rereading them in *The
Collected Shorter Poems*, less by their stylistic and philosophical
complexity than by the persistent anguish of mutability, the loss
of love, the inevitability of death. The direct statement of "The
Thin Edge of Your Pride" and "Confusion"—love poems for
Leslie Smith and Nancy Shores—seems to me more moving and
enduring than the Cubist poems, which are by no means cold-
blooded. Even when Rexroth seems playful, as in "3 Local Men
Vanquish Monster in Fight," there are passages of genuine fear
and trembling:

> The flesh is thin on her cheeks like paper. Those
> who arrive will be confounded in her pale eyes.
> The grey swords will pass nothing will be
> asked of her they go to the unendurable torso
> and the gnawing mice.
> (44)

Of all the Cubist poems in *The Art of Worldly Wisdom,* "In the
Memory of Andrée Rexroth" (27), written after her death in
1940, strikes the most sustained elegiac note, for it is uncomplicated by the tragicomic absurdity that characterizes many of
the others. I have already considered these poems as expressions
of Rexroth's philosophical quest for transcendence out of despair,
and I do not mean to imply now that the ideas are unimportant;
but, with familiarity, the poems communicate more feeling than
thought. In context with the new poems of "Gödel's Proof," in
which Rexroth's anguish is so clear and uncomplicated, *The Art
of Worldly Wisdom* clearly expresses the emotions of personal
separation and loss. Out of these emotions, the dialectical quest
begins.

The same emotions, ache and fear, are communicated by
In What Hour (1940); but they have become generalized by
the historical tragedies of the 1930's. Some of the poems are
impersonal, oratorical, apocalyptic; but in the most characteristic
ones, Rexroth walks alone in fields, woods, or on mountains,
mourning the Spanish or Chinese dead as he watches stars move
across the sky. In such poems—"Requiem for the Spanish Dead"
(86), "Another Early Morning Exercise" (92), "Autumn in
California" (93), and others—his own loneliness and fear become
representative of the human condition:

> A chill comes over me; I walk along shivering;
> Thinking of a world full of miserable lives,
> And all the men who have been tortured
> Because they believed it was possible to be happy.
>
> (93)

As we move through *In What Hour,* revolutionary hopes give
way to political despair; whatever faith in history Rexroth once
had collapses, and he is left alone in nature, far from war but
always aware of it as an aspect of the universal process of destruction and loss—a process which mysteriously has a creative
dimension also. In "Toward an Organic Philosophy" we are
reminded of "Yin and Yang." The cycles of birth and death,
creation and destruction, discovery and loss are eternal; but
consciousness of this process does not ease the anguish, though
it ennobles it. Whatever value there is in life, Rexroth is saying,
is created through consciousness of loss, death, annihilation. As

in *The Art of Worldly Wisdom,* elegiac and tragic emotions are
fundamental.

Stylistically, however, Rexroth's poetry from 1920 to 1940 was
quite uneven, ranging from the Revolution of the Word to the
plain speech of poems in the tradition of the Greek Anthology
and Chinese and Japanese classics. In the short poems from
The Phoenix and the Tortoise (1944), which come next in *The
Collected Shorter Poems,* we find a mastery of direct statement.
Gone is the tortured diction of his Cubist experiments. Instead,
from the first poem, "When We with Sappho" (139), to the last,
"Past and Future Turn About" (168), there is consistent clarity
of language. Mutability, periodicity, the universal process of
creation and destruction are revealed in poem after poem in
which the ecstasy of erotic union—brief though it may be—is
celebrated, both in its present immediacy and in memory. The
value of love is heightened by its brevity, by the brevity of life
itself. Poems of joyful fulfillment are balanced by elegies for his
wife and mother, by poems of separation and loneliness, and by
tragic reminders of war. He is saved from despair by a kind of
erotic and matrimonial mysticism in which he finds himself
participating in the natural cycles, in the "annual and diurnal
patterns" (163). In the Duality of love—the "I-Thou"—he has
found his place in the universe. With equanimity, he can imagine
his own death—his "still glowing ashes" (164).

This equanimity also characterizes *The Signature of All Things*
(1950), poems in which he continues to celebrate communion
with nature and those he loves—his living wife Marie, his dead
wife Andrée, his mother Delia, his poet-friends William Carlos
Williams, Yvor Winters, and Brother Antoninus. The title poem,
in which, like Boehme, he sees "the world as streaming/ In the
electrolysis of love" (177), is possibly the finest of his short
visionary reveries. In it, the integral person floats free of sin,
evil, time, death. And as we have seen, in "A Letter to William
Carlos Williams" (193), Rexroth shows with great purity and
directness how a poet "creates/ Sacramental relationships/ That
last always" (195). Without saying so, Rexroth has done precisely this in these poems. The purity of their language, the clarity
of their vision, and the rich consistency of their tone contribute
to the perfect unity of this book.

In order to maintain the quiet tone, Rexroth has reprinted
from *The Dragon and the Unicorn* (1952) only passages that

are musically descriptive in the next section of *The Collected Shorter Poems*. None is satirical, polemical, or dialectical, although most of the long poem (reprinted in its entirety in *The Collected Longer Poems* has these qualities. Moreover, only two excerpts in *The Collected Shorter Poems* are from his European travels—"Rosa Mundi," in which "Bright petals of evening/ Shatter, fall, drift over Florence" (215) and in "Golden Section" (218), a meditation on Roman ruins. The other six excerpts are from Part V of the long poem, in which he returns to California— to Golden Gate Park, to rivers and canyons, to the mountain cottage where he and Andrée were poor and/ Happy together" (222) two decades before. Here he reflects, "As long as we are lost/ In the world of purpose/ We are not free" (223). As he looks into the fire, he remembers the wars and adventures he used to imagine there, the life he had dreamed of living. "Now I see only fire" (223). He is free from the world of purpose.

Turning to *In Defense of the Earth* (1956), we find a development of this theme of visionary self-discovery in "The Reflecting Trees of Being and Not Being" (227). Love and loneliness in Europe and California continue to be subjects for some of his poems ("She Is Away" [228] and others in the sequence originally titled "For Marthe"); and the quiet elegiac tone that had characterized much of *The Phoenix and the Tortoise, The Signature of All Things*, and the excerpts from *The Dragon and the Unicorn* pervades *In Defense of the Earth*, poems for his wife and children and revolutionary friends, poems about "The Bad Old Days" of his adventurous youth, poems of organic communion, until the rage of "Thou Shalt Not Kill" (267) breaks the mood.

In this poem, it is as if the anarchistic prophet had returned to confront the cold-war enemies of mankind after a quiet exile in the mountains, or as if, recalling the revolutionary vows of his youth, he feels driven by desperation to denounce "the century of horror" (275). The poem is essential for understanding Rexroth's total personality, and it helps unite the contemplative-visionary qualities of the poetry of his middle age with the revolutionary themes and moods of *In What Hour*. Rage gives way to the playful, but cutting, satire of "A Bestiary" and the "Mother Goose" poems for his daughters; and, after some epigrams, translations, and satires, the book ends with the pair of philosophical statements called "They Say This Isn't a Poem" (312) and "Codicil" (314). The book lacks the extraordinary unity of *The Signa-*

ture of All Things, but it does show the tougher dimensions of
his personality that are played down in the earlier book, and it
is his most comprehensive treatment of his family, his children,
as well as of his own childhood.

The new poems of *Natural Numbers* (1964) continue to explore
the same themes—his children, his youth, love, loneliness, organic
communion. There are a couple of satires, but rage has given
way to resignation, and most of the poems are elegiac. Several
poems, written for music by Ornette Coleman and Eric Satie,
have a cool lyricism, and the book ends with a quiet sequence of
love poems called "Air and Angels" (338). In style and tone,
the conclusion of *The Collected Shorter Poems* harmonizes with
the new poems at the beginning. The cycle is complete.

In reviewing *The Collected Shorter Poems,* John Unterecker
surveyed Rexroth's development "from egotism to social awareness" and thence to a "more honest . . . still terribly public . . .
self-analysis. . . . In the late poems, we become nearly participants in the drama of Rexroth's career."[4] It seems to me odd
that Unterecker would use "egotism' to describe *The Art of
Worldly Wisdom;* for the Cubist poems in that volume are among
Rexroth's most impersonal, objectivist work. Moreover, the philosophical dimension of his poetry prevents it from being merely
autobiographical or self-centered. The drama of his life is, I
believe, successfully universalized.

The poet William Stafford worte a more perceptive review of
the volume:

To start with what may be a very naïve observation: all his life
Rexroth has apparently carried a burden that would seem quixotic
to many writers with less swagger and less voiced recklessness—he
has worked a tradition that puts forward poems that try to tell the
truth. Even the determined imagism of many of the poems conveys
an air of not wanting to claim more than what *is.* . . . There is a
strange irony in the best poems, . . . typified by the lament for
Thomas: they succeed best when they take off and become untrue.
No one in a Brooks Brothers suit killed Dylan, as the poem so
emphatically asserts; but the intensity of the lie makes a good poem.[5]

Stafford understands perfectly what kind of poetry Rexroth has
devoted his life to writing—a poetry of fact rather than of fantasy,
invention, construction for the sake of beauty, or art for art's
sake. Rexroth believes that value resides in fact as man experiences it. To separate value from fact, as many Western philoso-

phers have done from Plato to the Logical Positivists, is, in his view, to dehumanize ideas and experience, to make ideas appear to be distinct from experience. Through poetry Rexroth discovers value in a world of facts, and in this sense his wisdom is "worldly."

Stafford knows this intent; and yet, surprisingly, he reads "Thou Shalt Not Kill" as a poetic lie, successful because of its intensity, rather than as the poem that Rexroth tried to write. If on the surface it does not seem to be true, we should, I think, search for a deeper truth. If the men in Brooks Brothers suits, organization men of depersonalized society, did not literally kill Thomas, it is nevertheless true that a suicidal dream of success drove him on to the point where his vision could not save him. Rexroth calls for each of us to assume responsibility for Thomas' death, for the death of all the young men—to recognize our own involvement in, and dependence upon, the culture of death. The prophetic accusation should be taken as a kind of truth, as Rexroth intends it, rather than as a lie that makes for good poetry, in Oscar Wilde's sense. Perhaps the clichés of the 1950's and the shrill rhetoric obscure the truth. Perhaps Rexroth's terroristic inclinations—"I want to strangle your children at their finger paintings" (274)—obscure the moral impact of his anger. Certainly the poem is flawed. But it should not be read, I think, for "intensity" apart from truth. If it is false, let it be rejected instead of being praised for qualities that Rexroth did not intend. The implication of all of his work is that he would rather have it destroyed and forgotten than remembered as a beautiful lie.

Rexroth's prophetic and satirical poems have seldom been read with the seriousness that they deserve, even by his admirers, who sometimes seem embarrassed by them. If they praise these poems, they often do so as a stepping stone to others. Dudley Fitts, for example, has written: "It is not as a kind of latter-day Thersites, the continual complainer of things that are, that Mr. Rexroth will be remembered, but as the loving, wise celebrant of man in his relations with his fellows and with the earth that takes them all."[6] This forecast may be true, and Rexroth seems to want it to be true, if the omission of angry poems from *Natural Numbers* is any indication. Rexroth seems to be mellowing with age, writing fewer satires and including none from *The Dragon and the Unicorn* in *The Collected Shorter Poems*. But the fierce satires, the desperate protestations, the loud polemics are essential dimensions of his work and outlook. His moments of joyful transcendence have never come easily, as in Whitman's poetry; for they have emerged from a deep sensitivity to the horror of the modern world, from a hardheaded comprehension of the doom of history, from a lifelong struggle against despair. No affirmation has been possible without negation, and the poems of the negation and protest should not be neglected.

Neither should Rexroth's literary Cubism be discounted, for it represents a heroic effort to cope with despair. In this style, both serious and comic, he was searching for the seeds of transcendent vision in the elements of experience itself. He tried always to be true to his perception, analyzing it into discrete elements which he would then recombine, in the poem, in fresh juxtapositions. Concerning "the Revolution of the Word" in general, he once termed it "the most significant tendency in American literature,"[7] making it part of the international modernist movement in the 1920's but failing like other promising movements of "the generation of revolutionary hope." In the 1930's he perfected his style of direct statement, though he has written Cubist poems from time to time, such as the magnificent "Andromeda Chained to Her Rock the Great Nebula in Her Heart," at the beginning of *The Collected Shorter Poems* (3). It and "In the Memory of Andrée Rexroth" (27) seem to me to be the most deeply felt of the Cubist poems. His contribution to "the Revolution of the Word" is minor, in comparison with the work of Ezra Pound, Gertrude Stein, e. e. cummings, and T. S. Eliot; but his stylistic experiments helped him clarify his vision and language. It was a preparation for his more characteristic style of direct statement.

His poems in direct statement may be considered in several groups. There are personal elegies for his mother (153, 176), for Andrée (154, 166, 190), and for himself (164). Then there are elegies in which he mourns those who have died in wars and failed revolutions. "At Lake Desolation" (82) and "Hiking on the Coast Range" (84) are impersonal visions of death, whereas he is present in others, meditating on the dead as he walks under the stars. He commemorates those killed in the Spanish Civil War in "Requiem for the Spanish Dead' (86), victims of the Chinese Civil War in "Another Early Morning Exercise" (92), those Europeans who "fell like leaves/ In the autumn of nineteen thirty-nine" in "Falling Leaves and Early Snow" (109).

"white robed ski troops" in "Strength through Joy" (156-57), and Sacco and Vanzetti in "Climbing Milestone Mountain, August 22, 1937" (89) and "Fish Peddler and Cobbler" (318). And in "Un Bel di Vedremo" (158-59), he remembers his childhood before World War I as he listens to news of World War II: "It is a terrible thing to see a world die twice." These elegies of historical tragedy show the depths of Rexroth's response, which is the basis for his idea of "total liability" in *The Phoenix and the Tortoise* and *The Dragon and the Unicorn.*

Usually in the elegies, death is ennobled through consciousness of the eternal processes of creation and destruction, the cycles of nature. A few poems—"Yin and Yang" (23), "Adonis in Winter" (159), "Adonis in Summer" (160), and "Advent" (201)—treat these cycles rather impersonally; more typically, he is present, wandering through forests or on mountains as he contemplates "the changes of the weather,/ Flowers, birds, rabbits, mice and other small deer/ Fulfilling the year's periodicity" ("Precession of the Equinoxes," 154). The most lyrical of these poems of periodicity is, I think, "We Come Back," beginning, "Now, on this day of the first hundred flowers,/ Fate pauses for us in imagination" (163); the most philosophically developed in "Past and Future Turn About" (168); the most purely descriptive, "Toward an Organic Philosophy" (101). Other fine poems of this type are "The Wheel Revolves" (20), "Another Spring" (145), "It Rolls On" (152), and "Lyell's Hypothesis Again" (180). Other poems focus on the moment of organic vision in which the integral person is revealed in universality, liberated from time, space, the world. A sense of natural cycles, of creative process, is important in these poems, but the emphasis is on the poet's vision. "The Signature of All Things" (177), "Hojoki" (187), "Empty Mirror" (223), "Doubled Mirrors" (224), and "Time Is the Mercy of Eternity" (247) are among the best poems of personal transcendence, though passages of many other poems communicate the experience.

Organic vision, the sense of creative process, and awareness of the inevitability of death also permeate love poems such as "When We with Sappho" (139), his most passionate and eloquent, as well as "Lute Music" (143), "Floating" (144), "Incarnation" (162), "Theory of Numbers" (164), "Between Myself and Death" (175), "She Is Away" (228), "The Old Song and Dance" (231), and "A Dialogue of Watching" (259). There are also three sequences that mourn the separation of lovers: 'Time Is an Inclusion Series Said McTaggart" (12), "The Thin Edge of Your Pride" (31), and "Inversely, As the Square of Their Distances Apart" (148). Poems for and about his children include the sequences "The Lights in the Sky Are Stars" (237), "Mary and the Seasons" (260), "Bestiary" (276), and "Mother Goose" (285). These poems of love, marriage, and his family show more convincingly than do the longer, philosophical poems how erotic and matrimonial mysticism saved him from despair. In them, "I-Thou" is not a theory but a fact; and responsibility is actual, tangible communion. Significantly, he has placed poems about his children in close proximity to poems that center on his own youth: "Only Years" (222), "A Living Pearl" (234), "For Eli Jacobson" (244), and "The Bad Old Days" (258).

Three outstanding poems express his poetics of visionary communion—"August 22, 1939" (97), "A Letter to William Carlos Williams" (193), and "Codicil" (314). A pair of poems called "They Say This Isn't a Poem" (312) present the pernicious philosophy of objective order ("stinking with the blood/ Of wars and crucifixions") in contrast to his own, and Homer's, Personalism, in which the only order is "a reflection/ Of the courage, loyalty,/ Love, and honesty of men" (313). I am not competent to judge the accuracy of his translations, but certainly his modification of "The Epitaph at Corinth" for Andrée (25), "The Great Canzon," adapted from Dante's, for Marthe (232), "Martial —XII, LII" for Marie (164), and "Lucretius, III, 1053-1076" (202), number among the most eloquent poems of this volume, which ranks honorably among the collected short poems of America's best poets. The range of thought and feeling, from some of the most passionate love poems in American literature to elegies for mass destruction, is amazing; and the organic vision that unifies the collection establishes Rexroth in the tradition of Emerson, Thoreau, Whitman, Dickinson, and Frost, just as his experimentalism places him among such modernists as Gertrude Stein, T. S. Eliot, Ezra Pound, Wallace Stevens, e. e. cummings, and William Carlos Williams. Before determining his place in these traditions, however, we must turn to the longer poems.

II   The Heart's Garden/ The Garden's Heart

Rexroth's most recent long poem, *The Heart's Garden/ The Garden's Heart* (1967), is a masterpiece of visionary communion

with nature and the Tao, or the Way. Written in Kyoto during his world tour in 1967, it was published the same year by the Pym-Randall Press, and reprinted the following year in *The Collected Longer Poems.*
It begins with the aging poet wandering through Japanese forests at the beginning of summer. He hears the music of water and wind, but he is "listening/ Deep in his mind to music/ Lost far off in space and time" (CLP, 283). He recalls Lao Tzu's imagery of the Tao: "The valley's soul is deathless./ It is called the dark woman./ The dark woman is the gate/ To the root of heaven and earth" (283).[8] The Eternal Way is characterized by quietness and passivity: "She is possessed without effort" (283). But he feels toward the Tao like a man who has lost the woman he loves. He does not know how to find her. He does not know where he is, who he is, what he has done, what he can hope for (184); and yet he is aware that the desire for vision is self-defeating, for "visions are/ The measure of the defect/ Of vision" (185). Illumination is innocence, a kind of ignorance: "The illuminated live/ Always in light and so do/ Not know it is there as fishes/ Do not know they live in water" (285). The Tao is like light, but is unseen, just as it is like music, but unheard. To find the Tao, one must stop looking for it; for true vision is free from desire: "He who lives without gasping/ Lives always in experience/ Of the immediate as the/ Ultimate" (294-95).
Aware of the dangers of seeking the Tao, he discovers it in sensuous communion with nature. Seeing "Yellow rice blades in blue water" (283), "white stars/ Of dwarf iris" (285), "Gold leaves of feather bamboo" (286), "Gold fish . . . red/ As fire" (286), "The smoke/ And mist of the waterfall" (285), hearing the waterfall, birds, birdlike voices of women, a temple bell and gong, "K'oto meadows, samisen/ Lakes, mountain drums" (283), smelling incense and perfume of flowers and forest, he loses himself in sensations that blend with increasing richness as the poem unwinds:

> The sound of gongs, the songs of birds,
> The chanting of men, floating wisps
> Of incense, drifting pine smoke,
> Perfume of the death of spring—
> The warm breeze clouds the mirror
> With the pollen of the pines,
> And thrums the strings of the lute. (302)

The Tao, however, though it is in the sensed world, is not itself sensed. Observing a waterfall, he is aware that "Something moves reciprocally/ To the tumbling water." "It speaks in the molecules/ Of your blood, in the pauses/ Between your breathing"; and this something, the Tao, is an "invisible light" (109), an unheard music, the wholeness and harmony of experience. In his wanderings over mountains and through valleys conversing with tree frogs, bathed with delight, hearing the click of looms and the clinks of pachinko pinball machines—"the random/ Ticking of organic time" (296)—he receives "The reward of right contemplation": satori, or enlightenment. In the following passage, "it" has no referent; but the "something" or Tao is assumed. He attains

> The revelation that it is all
> Gravel and moss and rocks and clipped
> Shrubbery. That it doesn't
> Symbolize anything at all.
> The birds are quite aware
> Of its meaning. They ignore
> Monastery walls and are
> Furiously mating everywhere
> In the hot perfumed sunlight.
>
> (297)

Seeing things as they are, his mind free from illusion, his heart free from grasping. Rexroth seems to have attained satori as described by the Zen Buddhist Seigen Ishin: "Before a man studies Zen, to him mountains are mountains and waters are waters; after he gets an insight into the truth of Zen through the instruction of a good master, mountains to him are not mountains and waters are not waters; but after this when he really attains to the abode of rest, mountains are once more mountains and waters are waters."[9] To the enlightened eye, everything is holy—the most ordinary object, such as a stone or uncarved block of wood, being no less sacred than a temple. Similarly, any human act may be regarded as worship: the "Prostitute worships in her/ Own way all through the white night" (299).

Rexroth's visionary communion with the Tao is achieved in language which is as sensuous as the perceptions it conveys. In fact, no poem of Rexroth's is as musically rich, with the exception of his first long poem, *The Homestead Called Damas-*

cus. Just as in *The Collected Shorter Poems* he circled back to the feelings of his youth, so in *The Heart's Garden/ The Garden's Heart* he regains the pure harmonies of his earliest style. The language, however, has become simplified. The scientific and philosophical vocabulary of his early work is missing from his latest work. Rather than theorizing about vision, he conveys it directly. In a very real sense, the poem *is* the vision; for the sounds and silences of speech unify the poet's sensations. The unity, the harmony, of speech and perception *is* the Tao.

> The Eve of Ch'ing Ming—Clear Bright,   1
> A quail's breast sky and smoky hills,   2
> The great bronze gong booms in the   3
> Russet sunset. Late tonight   4
> It will rain. Tomorrow will   5
> Be clear and cool once more. One more   6
> Clear, bright day in this floating life.   7
> (294)

How simple, yet how rich, the sound, how intricate the patterns that make for harmony. The first five lines, like most of the lines in the poem, are of seven syllables each; but the five stresses in each of the first two lines make them seem long and languid in contrast to the abruptness of the fourth and fifth lines. The indecisive ending of the third line and, in the fourth, the internal rhyme ("Russet sunset"), the alliterative *s*'s and *t*'s, and the caesura contribute to the change of pace; and the sixth and seventh lines are a return to the languidness which is a characteristic of the "floating life."

Patterns of vowels and consonants are also important in giving the poem contour. First there are three stressed *ee*'s and internal rhyme: "The Eve of Ch'ing Ming." "Clear Bright"—the name of the day which prophetically describes the day—is repeated in the last line, and "clear" is also in the sixth. "Breast," "bronze," and "booms" alliterate with "Bright"; "tonight" rhymes with it; and the *i*'s in "sky" and "life" provide additional linkage. Playing against the *i*'s are the low resonances of the *o*'s and *u*'s in "smoky," "bronze gong booms," "Russet sunset," "tonight" and "Tomorrow," "cool once more. One more," and "floating." The *t*'s of "Bright," "breast," "great," "russet sunset. Late tonight," "tomorrow," and, repeated in the last line, "bright" lead to "floating"; and the *f* and *l* reappear in "life."

Such patterns are, of course, not mechanical, and if they do not occur in the poetic utterance itself—in the speech act—no analysis will reveal them. For Rexroth, the poem is the act itself; music is in the human voice, not in an abstract pattern. The poem must be heard or read aloud for the "floating life" to be manifested. Just as the most ordinary object is holy to the enlightened eye, the most ordinary words become an amazing music in this poem.

III   The Collected Longer Poems

Rexroth's major accomplishments as a philosophical poet are the plays, *Beyond the Mountains,* and *The Collected Longer Poems* (1968). "Written between five and ten years apart," he tells us in his introduction to the latter volume, published by New Directions in 1968, "all the sections of this book now seem to me almost as much one long poem as do *The Cantos* or *Paterson*."[10] He notes that some shorter philosophical poems—such as "The Thin Edge of Your Pride," "When You Asked for It Did You Get It," "Organon," "Ice Shall Cover Nineveh," and "Past and Future Turn About"—might be considered "in temporal sequence" with the longer poems, and that "Most poets resemble Whitman in one respect—they write only one book and that an interior autobiography." The principal phases of his spiritual development are clearly charted in the Damascan brothers' quest for transcendence through love and martyrdom in *Homestead,* in the apocalyptic Christian vision of *Prolegomenon,* in the acceptance of universal responsibility through sacramental marriage in *The Phoenix and the Tortoise,* in the recognition of reality itself as "a community of lovers" in *The Dragon and the Unicorn,* and finally in the Taoist-Zen Buddhist illumination of *The Heart's Garden/ The Garden's Heart,* in which "The real objects are their own transcendental meaning."

"Today Kenneth Rexroth has moved from experiment to consolidation," Lawrence Lipton wrote in a review of *The Collected Longer Poems.* "From questing and discovery to reappraisals and summations. . . . Rexroth's position in twentieth century American poetry is secure. He is a major poet of the greatest gifts. . . ."[11] Other critics would, of course, at this date, disagree—and some violently. Rexroth has been praised by some as a poet of love and nature; by others as an elegist and translator; by still others as a satirist, polemicist, and man of ideas; but by very few for the totality of his work. Often he has been admired more for *what* he says than for *how well* he says it.

Robert Stock, for example, praising the revolutionary philosophy of love in *The Collected Longer Poems,* concluded that it is "significant primarily for extra-poetic reasons."[12] The charge is not new, for even Rexroth's friend William Carlos Williams once wrote in a letter to Marianne Moore, concerning *The Phoenix and the Tortoise,* that "It is not very subtly made as far as the phrasing, the words, the godliness of words is concerned, but its impelling reason is surprisingly refreshing if one has the hardihood to go on reading—and is not thrown over the horse's head by the exhuberance (is that the way to spell it?) of the beast. Rexroth is no writer in the sense of the word-man. For him words are sticks and stones to build a house—but it's a good house."[13]

Of course, Williams objected in principle to abstract diction in poetry, so he is not the best judge of Rexroth's often eloquent dialectics. And it must be added that, when Rexroth's diction is sensuous, the "sticks and stones" of common speech become foci of illumination like Lao Tzu's uncarved block: "FIRE/ The air is dizzy with swallows" (CLP, 172), for instance, or "Each twig/ Is tipped with buds, deep crimson,/ Overlaid with fine black lines/ Like drops of congealing blood" (268). Elsewhere, Williams has paid high compliments to the "pith" and "jolt" of the style of *Beyond the Mountains,*[14] to the musicality of the Chinese translations—"his ear is finer than that of anyone I have ever encountered"—and to the brilliance of the satires.[15]

Richard Eberhart, responding more enthusiastically to the style of *The Dragon and the Unicorn,* wrote that "The lines are hard and clear, precise and lean, with continuous tensile strength and nothing fuzzy."[16] And Richard Foster, summing up Rexroth's achievement, has called him "a fine lyric poet whose work has affinities with much of the best lyric poetry of the past. He is no barbaric yawper, as I had formerly believed."[17] In my opinion, the great range of Rexroth's style, from intellectually tough polemics and satires to heartbreakingly tender elegies, from Cubist innovations to the sensuous passion of plain statement, from the dynamic dialogue of *Beyond the Mountains* to the visionary musicality of *The Heart's Garden/ The Garden's Heart,* establishes him as a "word-man" of the first rank.

Rexroth's words are not merely elements of poetic construction; they are the light of living speech, from person to person. Rexroth is a visionary poet like Blake, Whitman, Yeats, Lawrence, Thomas, and Ginsberg. Vision may mean sensuous perception, which is an important aspect of his poetry; and it may also mean a philosophical outlook, a Weltanschauung; but the central meaning of "vision" in Rexroth's writings is spiritual illumination, enlightenment, Zen satori, the Quaker Inner Light, Buber's "I-Thou" communion, the source of human communication and community. For Rexroth, vision is actuality: "it is precisely the thing in itself that we do experience," he states in the introduction to the CLP; and in a recent interview: "our experience of reality begins and ends in illumination."[18]

His visionary poetry should be judged, therefore, not primarily in terms of construction, or invention, or stylistic qualities, but in terms of how well it conveys this "experience of reality." Obviously, judgment of mystical poetry is even more subjective than judgments of esthetic form and technique. Fortunately, Rexroth has made a helpful remark: "Actually, mystical poetry communicates a kind of trance state, an emptiness which is a state of not grasping. The creation of such poetry is like the slow development of a state of bliss in which grasping disappears."[19] Reading it, we experience loss of ego, will, and self-consciousness similar to that experienced by the poet; for reader and poet unite in an "I-Thou." It seems to me that "The Signature of All Things," *The Heart's Garden/ The Garden's Heart,* and other poems by Rexroth communicate the "trance state" as profoundly as Yeats's "To the Rose upon the Rood of Time" or "The Cold Heaven."

An important problem in Rexroth's work is the relation between visionary communion and the abstract thought of his Weltanschauung. Each of the longer poems, Rexroth goes on to explain in his introduction, is "a philosophical revery—but a revery in dialogue in which philosophies come and go." Direct sensuous vision is the central experience of his work, and his search for a rationale in abstract terms never ends in certainty, for ideas are always approximations and to some extent illusory. Apparently, he has been suspicious of conceptualization, despite his great proclivity for it, ever since his boyhood when he turned to philosophy for an understanding of visionary experience that was not explained by scientific materialism. According to *An*

Autobiographical Novel, "Gradually I discovered that philosophy, certainly philosophy since the Middle Ages, has never made anyone wiser or happier, and that the most extensive acquaintance with, and habit of, philosophical speculation has never imparted an iota of wisdom to anyone. Still, that sense of exaltation, that feeling of being on the brink of discovering the Absolute, is really a habit of living. I formed it then and never lost it and I am not sorry, although I have long since ceased to believe that there is anything to discover which doesn't meet the naked eye."[20]

This statement is not entirely convincing, for certainly much of *The Dragon and the Unicorn,* for instance, reads as if it is intended to be true, both as fact and idea. In *The Heart's Garden/The Garden's Heart,* on the other hand, abstract philosophizing has diminished to the point at which there is very little tension between idea and experience. It seems to me that, for much of his life, Rexroth has been haunted by the desire for ideas that are true, though they turn out, ultimately, to be merely beautiful. *Merely* beautiful? Perhaps beauty is the ultimate value after all. To return to his discussion of his boyhood in *An Autobiographical Novel:* "What I was learning, of course, is that philosophy is a work of art; the best philosophers were the ones who wrote best; the best systems were the prettiest. Nothing could be less like the real world than Plato's *Timaeus,* or Leibniz's *Monadology,* or McTaggart's timeless, spaceless universe of love. Their virtues are of the same order as a fugue or a Cubist painting."[21]

Rexroth seems to have come to the conclusion of the young Yeats "that whatever of philosophy has been made poetry is alone permanent."[22] George Santayana came to a similar conclusion in his discussion of Lucretius, Dante, and Goethe: "the vision of philosophy is sublime. The order it reveals in the world is something beautiful, tragic, sympathetic to the mind, and just what every poet, on a small or on a large scale, is always trying to catch."[23] Rexroth, of course, denies that philosophy reveals order that is objectively in the world, but he would agree with Santayana that "contemplation is imaginative.... A philosopher who attains it is, for the moment, a poet; and a poet who turns his practiced and passionate imagination on the order of all things, or on anything in the light of the whole, is for that moment a philosopher."[24]

Susanne Langer's claim for philosophical poetry, which is less grandiose than Santayana's, is based on its creation of "the *semblance* of reasoning, the seriousness, strain, and progress, conviction, and acceptance—the whole experience of philosophical thinking."[25] Her emphasis on experience would appeal to Rexroth, though he would quibble with "semblance," which implies that genuine philosophical thinking is not in the poem itself. Closer to Rexroth's view is that of Denis Saurat, literary critic and historian of science, who argues that one function of philosophical poetry is to reveal the "artistic truth" of metaphysical ideas that are not literally true but which express man's being in the universe.[26] This view is considerably more subtle than that of William Stafford, who in praising the intensity of "lie" of "Thou Shalt Not Kill" missed the deeper truth expressed in that prophetic poem, as we have seen. For Rexroth, the truth of poetry resides in its being an act of communion, communication, community. He clearly belongs in the tradition of sensuous visionaries—Spenser, Milton, Goethe, Hugo, Nietzsche, Blake, and Whitman—which Saurat discusses in terms of such basic ideas as the sexual nature of creation and the mutual responsibility of all beings.

As a philosophical poet for whom poetry is vision and philosophy is an art, what is Rexroth's relation to other modern American poets? According to L. S. Dembo, much of their work rests on "the view that art is a medium for 'knowing' the world in its 'essentiality,' for apprehending things as they are. . . . In such a theory, as one can readily deduce, 'knowledge' becomes indistinguishable from aesthetic emotion."[27] The more specific doctrine of Objectivism, he goes on to say, has guided much of the work of e. e. cummings, Hart Crane, Ezra Pound, T. S. Eliot, Marianne Moore, William Carlos Williams, Wallace Stevens, Charles Olson, and Robert Duncan. The Objectivist thesis is "that art must be directed toward the object and not the subject, that the artist must attain what Leconte de Lisle called *impassibilité*, in which one escapes the tyranny of 'personal caprice and taste,' the *angoisse du coeur et de ses voluptés*."[28]

Rexroth, on the contrary, has insisted that poetry communicates "things as they are" by virtue of its Personalism. He has generally opposed Objectivism as Dembo analyzes it: "Pronouncements of the Imagists, Williams' famous principle 'No ideas but in things,' Stevens' 'The world must be measured by eye,' Crane's notion of poetic 'surrender' to the object, and similar theories in other poets, are symptomatic of an objectivist way of looking at experience in general and the function of poetry in particular."[29] Rexroth has pointed out in his poem "Codicil" that, "If vigorously enough/ Applied, such a theory/ Produces in practice its/ Opposite": "intense,/ Subjective revery" (CSP, 314). Of course, his poetry shares some of the characteristics of Objectivism—definite imagery of precise visual perception, for instance, and a feeling of "surrender" but, in theory as well as in much of his poetry, he has countered Objectivism with Personalism, in which "objects are only perspectives on persons" (introduction to CLP) and poetry is personal vision, communion, communication, communal sacrament. It is true that Rexroth looks outward as he looks inward, and that he objectifies his experience in poetry; but he never hesitates to use the pronoun "I." Moreover, he opposes the Objectivist idealization and purification of language as a thing-in-itself, which, according to Dembo, characterizes modern American neo-epics such as Pound's *Cantos,* Crane's *Bridge,* Eliot's *Four Quartets,* and Williams' *Paterson.* It is too bad that Dembo omits mention of Rexroth, not only as a critic of Objectivism, but as a contributor to the American neo-epic; for in a fundamental respect his sequence of philosophical reveries are like other long poems by American poets since Whitman, in which "the poet has become his own hero."[30]

Roy Harvey Pearce, upon whose *Continuity of American Poetry* Dembo has drawn for his conception of the modern poet as hero of the neo-epic, has concluded—after surveying Williams' *Paterson,* Crane's *Bridge,* Pound's *Cantos,* Whitman's *Leaves of Grass,* and Joel Barlow's *Columbiad* of 1807—that "the American poet again and again imaged himself—in Emerson's and Whitman's word—as an Adam who, since he might well be one with God, was certainly one with all men."[31] Pearce might well have included Rexroth, whose conception of himself as integral person in visionary communion with nature and mankind, for which he feels totally responsible, is as Adamic as Whitman's. In the "I-Thou" of love, the individual becomes universal; and the universe becomes paradisal.

Ever since Rexroth wrote *The Homestead Called Damascus* as a youth, he has deliberately worked in the tradition of "long philosophical reveries which are so characteristic of modern American poetry"; he lists, for example, the "Symphonies" of Conrad Aiken and John Gould Fletcher, Eliot's *The Waste Land,*

Pound's *Cantos*, Williams' *Paterson*, Zukofsky's *Poem Beginning "A,"* Walter Lowenfels' *Some Deaths,* and Parker Tyler's *Granite Butterfly*.[32] More than other American neo-epic poets, with the exception of Whitman and Williams, Rexroth emerges in his poems as himself, speaking directly to us; whereas in Pound's *Cantos* or in Eliot's *Waste Land,* for example, there is always a literary veil between poet and reader. Rexroth's personality develops throughout *The Collected Longer Poems.* He speaks to us directly as the wry narrator of *Homestead,* as his skeptical and sacrificial tendencies conflict in Thomas and Sebastian. Finding faith in *Prolegomenon,* he speaks as an apocalyptic Christian prophet. Debating major philosophical issues with himself in *The Phoenix and the Tortoise,* he discovers universal responsibility in marriage. As the man of the world in *The Dragon and the Unicorn,* he continues the debate across America and Europe, returning always to the visionary experience of love. As the aging sage in *The Heart's Garden/ The Garden's Heart,* he expresses "the immediate as the/ Ultimate" (CLP, 294-95). And in the two short poems that conclude the volume—"A Song at the Winepresses," for Gary Snyder, and "The Spark in the Tinder of Knowing," for James Laughlin—he celebrates "Reality enclosed in the heart,/ I and not I, the one/ In the Other, the Other/ In the One, the Holy Wedding" (307).

The person is vision; vision is reality; reality is communion and community. "If we ever get to the point of knowing how to define ourselves as persons," Pearce has written, "perhaps we will be able to define our community. Perhaps it will prove to be a community not with one image of the hero but with many— a community whose heroes' heroism consists in the fact that they can teach us how to resist a community's inevitable urge to coalesce all its heroes into one."[33] Rexroth's Personalism, his commemoration of a vast variety of visionaries, revolutionaries, poets, lovers, friends, and martyrs, and his courageous revelation of himself are major contributions to that end.

Rexroth's development has been a lifetime struggle against the dehumanizing forces of the twentieth century. From childhood bliss before World War I he fell into "experience"—the loss of family and community. *The Collected Longer Poems* records his painful struggle to regain the paradisal state, and it seems to be achieved in *The Heart's Garden / The Garden's Heart,* in which the "wanderer" "returns to Penelope" (303). Satire and polemics, such as those bitter sections of *The Dragon and the Unicorn*, have been essential expressions of the Adamic struggle against political, technological, and cultural forces of self-alienation. In discussing other neo-epic poets, Pearce writes that the Adamic impulse "thrusts against a culture made by Americans who come more and more to be frightened by it, even as they realize that it is basic to the very idea of their society: one (in Whitman's words) of simple, separate persons, yet democratic, en-masse."[34]

Of all the neo-epic poets, Rexroth has been the most explicitly anarchistic, the most revolutionary in his attack on militarism and war, bureaucracy and authoritarian politics, impersonal collectivities, and dehumanizing technology. His prophetic radicalism has been positive as well as negative in its affirmation of love and community as the essentials of the good society. Robert Stock has written recently that "What is most viable in the so-called New Left is in large part the creation of Rexroth and Paul Goodman whether the movement knows it or not. Young radicals might well go to this new collection of Rexroth's poems for the rediscovery and definition of their motives."[35]

For these writers, "I-Thou" is the source of humanistic revolution. Rexroth was active during the 1920's in the Industrial Workers of the World and during the 1930's in the John Reed Clubs; since World War II, he has turned from action more and more to contemplation—not because he has repudiated revolutionary values—but because, "When the light of contemplation goes out, the civilization collapses, and there is a kind of ecological point of no-return. . . . The interrelatedness of contemplatives is a skeleton or web which holds the social body. There is a critical point when there isn't enough of this web. We have long since reached that and passed it in America, and the society goes completely to pieces, however healthy it may seem. And of course the participants in the society violently deny that this is happening."[36] Action is, therefore, irrelevant; but he sympathizes with youth rebellion and "counter culture."

Among modern American neo-epic poets, Rexroth is at once the most revolutionary, the most philosophically disciplined and comprehensive, and the most erotically passionate. The Person of the poet is incomplete without female "Thous." "Marichi, an avatar of the Shakti of Shiva," Rexroth explains in his introduction to *The Collected Longer Poems*, "has three heads: a sow, a woman in orgasm, and the Dawn. 'Goddess of the Dawn,' as Westerners call her, her chariot drawn by swine, she haunts 'The Homestead Called Damascus' and comes back as a beautiful Communist girl in 'The Heart's Garden'—as does Vega, the jewel in the Lyre, the Weaving Girl who weaves and ravels and weaves again." In the "vicarity" of love—the I as Thou, the Thou as I—the Person experiences Paradise. In the heart's garden lies the garden's heart.

Notes and References

Chapter One

1. Preface to the 1802 edition of *Lyrical Ballads,* by William Wordsworth, edited by H. Littlefield (London, 1911), p. 237.

2. "Unacknowledged Legislators and 'Art Pour Art,'" *Bird in the Bush: Obvious Essays* (New York, 1959), pp. 16 and 5. Compare Williams' "Writer's Prologue to a Play in Verse" in *The Collected Later Poems* (New York, 1963), p. 13: "Would it disturb you if I said/ you have no other speech than poetry?"

3. *The Portable James Joyce* (New York, 1959), pp. 481-82.

4. T. S. Eliot, *Selected Essays, 1917-1932* (New York, 1932), pp. 7 and 11.

5. *An Autobiographical Novel* (New York, 1966), p. x.

6. W. C. Williams, *Paterson* (New York, 1951), p. 14.

7. Introduction to D. H. Lawrence, *Selected Poems* (New York, 1959), p. 11.

8. "The Heart's Garden / The Garden's Heart," *Collected Longer Poems* (New York, 1968), p. 285.

9. Introduction to the CLP, n.p.

10. *The Poetry and Prose of William Blake,* edited by David Erdman, Commentary by Harold Bloom (Garden City, New York, 1965), p. 481.

11. Martin Buber, *I and Thou* (New York, 1958), p. 11.

12. Richard Foster, "The Voice of the Poet: Kenneth Rexroth," *Minnesota Review,* II (1962), 382.

13. *Assays* (Norfolk, Connecticut, 1961), p. 57.

14. *An Autobiographical Novel* (Garden City, New York, 1966), p. 14.

15. *Ibid.,* p. 310.

16. *Selected Writings of Edward Sapir,* edited by David G. Mandelbaum (Berkeley and Los Angeles, 1949), p. 356.

17. Edward Sapir, *Language: an Introduction to the Study of Speech* (New York, 1921), p. 242.

18. *Ibid.,* p. 240.

19. René Wellek and Austin Warren, *Theory of Literature* (New York, 1956), p. 150.

20. *The Poetry and Prose of Walt Whitman,* edited by Louis Untermeyer (New York, 1949), p. 113.

21. Lawrence Lipton, "Notes Toward an Understanding of Kenneth

Rexroth with Especial Attention to 'The Homestead Called Damascus,'" *The Quarterly Review of Literature*, IX, 2 (1957), 37.

22. Jack Kerouac, *The Dharma Bums* (New York, 1958), pp. 11 and 13; see also p. 152. Contrast Kerouac's treatment with Mary McCarthy's portrayal of "the poet of the masses," Vincent Keogh, *The Groves of Academe* (New York, 1952), pp. 272-95. Though her prototype was undoubtedly Rexroth, she reveals nothing of his subtle imagination and sensibility. Keogh's conversation is crude to the point of being inept. For a sympathetic portrait of Rexroth, in verse, see John Ciardi's "One for Rexroth," *In Fact* (New Brunswick, New Jersey, 1962), p. 54. The poem was presented to Rexroth in celebration of his sixtieth birthday, during a symposium on "San Francisco's Cultural Future."

23. Leonard Kriegel, "Rexroth: Citizen of Bohemia," *The Nation*, CCII (June 6, 1966), 689.

24. Sarel Eimerl, "Compared with Me," *The Reporter*, XXXIV (May 19, 1966), 62.

25. Anonymous, "The Last Bohemian," *Time*, LVII (February 25, 1966), 108.

26. Henry Miller, *Tropic of Cancer* (Paris, n.d.), n.p.

27. James T. Farrell, *Studs Lonigan* (New York, 1938), pp. 140-47.

28. "Andrée Rexroth," *The Collected Shorter Poems* (New York, 1966), p. 154. See other elegies on pp. 166, 190, and 222.

29. Frederick J. Hoffman, "Sacco and Vanzetti as Leftist Heroes," *The Twenties: American Writing in the Postwar Decade* (New York, 1962), p. 403.

30. "Alienation," *Arts in Society*, VI, 1 (Spring-Summer, 1969), 59, reprinted as "Who Is Alienated from What?" *The Alternative Society: Essays from the Other World* (New York, 1970), p. 131.

31. "Samuel Beckett and the Importance of Waiting," *Bird in the Bush*, p. 84.

Chapter Two

1. "Notes," p. 39.

2. *Ibid.*, pp. 38-42.

3. "Voice," pp. 379-80.

4. Lawrence Lipton, "The Poetry of Kenneth Rexroth," *Poetry*, XC, 3 (June, 1957), 168-80.

5. Dorothe Van Ghent, Introduction, *Some Problems of Communication* (Oakland, California: Mills College Master's Thesis, 1935), 1-15. Inasmuch as she refers to Rexroth's poems in publications prior to *The Art of Worldly Wisdom*, I refer to the pagination of "Prolegomenon" in *The Collected Longer Poems*, pp. 37-60, and to other poems in *The Collected Shorter Poems*, pp. 25-78.

6. *Ibid.*, p. 94.

7. *Ibid.*, p. 109, quoted from Eliot's essay on "The Metaphysical Poets," *The Hogarth Essays* (Garden City, New York, 1928), p. 214.

8. Quoted by Van Ghent, p. 119, from T. S. Eliot's *The Sacred Wood*, 3rd edition (London, 1932), pp. 170-71.

9. *Some Problems*, p. 109.

10. *Ibid.*

11. *Ibid.*, p. 123.

12. Preface, *The Art of Worldly Wisdom* (Prairie City, Illinois, 1949), n.p.

13. "The Poetry of Kenneth Rexroth," p. 171.

14. C. M. Bowra, *Primitive Song* (New York, 1962), pp. 63-88.

15. Van Ghent, p. 116.

16. Bowra, p. 73.

17. William FitzGerald, "Twenty Years at Hard Labor," *Poetry*, LVII, 11 (November, 1940), 158.

18. Horace Gregory and Marya Zaturenska, *A History of American Poetry 1900-1940* (New York, 1946), p. 494.

19. Daniel Aaron, *Writers on the Left, Episodes in American Literary Communism* (New York, 1961), p. 341.

20. Rolfe Humphries, "Too Much Abstraction," *New Republic*, CIII (August 12, 1940), 221.

21. Foster, "Voice," p. 380.

22. Alexander Berkman, *The Bolshevik Myth* (New York, 1953); quoted passage reprinted in *The Anarchists*, edited by Irving L. Horowitz (New York, 1964), p. 506. See also James Joll's account of Kronstadt in *The Anarchists* (Boston, 1964), p. 191.

23. Introduction, *The Dragon and the Unicorn* (Norfolk, Connecticut, 1952), n.p.

Chapter Three

1. *The Complete Works of Shakespeare*, edited by Hardin Craig (Chicago, 1951), p. 464.

2. Foster, "Voice," p. 381.

3. *Ibid.*, p. 383.

4. Introduction, *Selected Poems of D. H. Lawrence* (New York, 1947; reprinted, New York, 1961), pp. 1-23—the pagination to which I shall refer. The essay, retitled "Poetry, Regeneration, and D. H. Lawrence," was included in *Bird in the Bush*, pp. 177-203.

5. Jacob Boehme, *The Signature of All Things* (London, 1934), p. 91.

6. *Ibid.*, p. 3.

7. Quoted by Evelyn Underhill in *Mysticism* (New York, 1961), p. 58.

8. Quoted by Sidney Spencer, *Mysticism in World Religion* (Baltimore, Maryland, 1963), p. 269.

9. Gordon K. Grigsby, "The Presence of Reality: The Poetry of Kenneth Rexroth," unpublished essay.

10. Selden Rodman, "Gnomic, Fastidious Verses," *New York Herald Tribune Book Review* (May 7, 1950), p. 22.

11. *Ibid.*

Chapter Four

1. *Beyond the Mountains* (New York, 1951). "Phaedra: A Dance Play" had originally appeared in *New Directions in Prose and Poetry*, IX (1946), pp. 156-86; *Iphigenia at Aulis* had been published in *Portfolio*, III (Spring, 1946), Leaf Five, 4 folio pages; and *Beyond the Mountains: A Dance Play* (later called "Hermaios") had been published in *The Quarterly Review of Literature*, IV, 3 (1948), 255-92.

2. W. C. Williams, "Verse with a Jolt to It," *New York Times Book Review* (January 28, 1951), p. 5.

3. W. B. Yeats, *Essays and Introductions* (London, 1961), p. 250.

4. Arthur Waley, Introduction, *The Nō Plays of Japan* (New York, n.d.), p. 21.

5. *Classics Revisited* (Chicago, 1968), p. 59.

6. "Introduction to *Hippolytus*," in *Euripides I,* translated and edited by David Grene and Richmond Lattimore (New York, 1967), p. 167. See also H. D. F. Kitto, *Greek Tragedy* (Garden City, N.Y., 1954), p. 213.

7. *Iphigenia in Aulis,* translated and with an Introduction by Charles R. Walker, in *The Complete Greek Tragedies,* Vol. IV: *Euripides* (Chicago, Illinois, 1959), pp. 361 and 370.

8. *The Collected Plays of W. B. Yeats* (New York, 1953), p. 364.

9. See "Amours de Voyage," written in 1849, in *The Poems of Arthur Hugh Clough,* edited by H. F. Lawry, A. L. P. Norrington, and F. L. Milhauser (Oxford, 1951), pp. 177-220, and Samuel Rogers' "Italy," *Poetical Works* (Philadelphia, 1866), pp. 221-451.

10. Dudley Fitts, "A Poet Abroad," *The New Republic* (February 9, 1953), 19.

11. Richard Eberhart, "A Voyage of the Spirit," *New York Times Book Review* (February 15, 1953), p. 25.

12. Rexroth modifies the biblical idea that "perfect love casteth out fear," 1 John 4:18 and Philippians 4:7.

Chapter Five

1. Thomas Parkinson, "Phenomenon or Generation," *A Casebook on the Beat,* edited by Parkinson (New York, 1961), pp. 281-83.

2. Kerouac, pp. 11 and 13.

3. Lawrence Ferlinghetti, "Horn on HOWL," *Evergreen Review,* I, 4 (1957), 153. For a brief article on the trial and illustrations of

Ginsberg, Rexroth, and other poets reading their work, see "Big Day for Bards at Bay," *Life*, XLIII, 2 (September 9, 1957), 105-8.

4. "San Francisco Letter," *Evergreen Review*, I, 2 (1957), 5.

5. *New World Writing*, 11 (New York, 1957), 28-41, reprinted in *A Casebook on the Beat*, pp. 179-93. The quotation appears on p. 181.

6. *Ibid.*, p. 191.

7. *Ibid.*, p. 193.

8. Introduction, *Bird in the Bush: Obvious Essays* (New York, 1959), p. ix.

9. "Revolt: True and False," *The Nation*, CLXXXVI (April 26, 1958), 378.

10. "Thar's Culture in Them Thar Hills," *New York Times Magazine* (February 7, 1965), p. 79.

11. Lawrence Lipton, "Rexroth," *The Los Angeles Free Press*, Part II (January 10, 1969), p. 23.

12. "A Sword in a Cloud of Light," *The Collected Shorter Poems*, p. 239.

13. R. W. Flint, "Poets and Their Subjects," *The New Republic*, CXXXVI (February 18, 1957), 19.

14. Muriel Rukeyser, "Lyrical 'Rage,'" *Saturday Review*, XL (November 9, 1957), p. 15.

15. M. L. Rosenthal, *The Modern Poets* (New York, 1960), pp. 165-66.

16. "Lament for the Makeris," *The Poems of William Dunbar*, edited by W. Mackay MacKenzie (London, 1932), p. 21.

17. W. C. Williams, "Two New Books by Kenneth Rexroth," *Poetry*, XC (June, 1957), 183.

18. *Ibid.*, p. 180.

19. Alfred Kazin, "Father Rexroth and the Beats," *The Reporter*, XXII (March 3, 1960), 54-56.

20. Richard Foster, "With Great Passion, a Kind of Person," *Hudson Review*, XIII, 1 (Spring, 1960), 149.

21. *Ibid.*, pp. 150-52.

22. Rexroth has had one-man shows of his paintings in Chicago, New York, Los Angeles, San Francisco, and Paris.

23. Parkinson, p. 282.

24. Foster, "With Great Passion," p. 151.

25. In using Marx's term "reification," Rexroth implies that capitalism militates against communism and community—an idea made explicit in *The Dragon and the Unicorn*. The Marxist philosopher Herbert Marcuse explains reification as follows:

> Marx's early writings are the first explicit statement of the process of reification (*Verdinglichung*) through which capitalist society makes all personal relations between men take

the form of objective relations between things. Marx expounds this process in his *Capital* as "the Fetishism of Commodities." The system of capitalism relates men to each other through the commodities they exchange. The social status of individuals, their standard of living, the satisfaction of their needs, their freedom, and their power are all determined by the value of their commodities. The capacities and needs of the individual have no part in the evaluation. Each man's most human attributes become a function of money, the general substitute of commodities.

Reason and Revolution: Hegel and the Rise of Social Theory (New York, 1954), p. 279. For Marx's theory of self-alienation and reification see especially his *Economic and Philosophic Manuscripts of 1844* (Moscow, 1959); Marx and Engels, *The German Ideology* (New York, 1947); and Marx's *Contribution to a Critique of Political Economy* (Chicago, 1904). An interpretation of alienation and state capitalism that helps clarify Rexroth's perspective is by Raya Dunayevskaya, *Marxism and Freedom . . . from 1776 until Today* (New York, 1958). See also my review, "Marx for Libertarians," *The Activist*, XIII (May 1965), 29-30, reprinted in *Anarchy*, LVII (November, 1965), 341-43.

26. Richard Foster, "Lucubrations of an Outside Insider," *The Minnesota Review*, III, 1 (Fall, 1962), 132.

27. *Ibid.*, pp. 132-33.

28. Foster, "With Great Passion," p. 152.

Chapter Six

1. Introduction, *The Signature of All Things* (New York, 1950), p. 10.

2. Lipton, "The Poetry of Kenneth Rexroth," pp. 174-75.

3. *Ibid.*, p. 177.

4. John Unterecker, "Calling the Heart to Order," *New York Times*, Section VII (July 23, 1967), p. 8.

5. William Stafford, "A Five Foot Shelf," *Poetry*, XI (December, 1967), 188.

6. Dudley Fitts, Untitled Note, *New York Times*, Section VII (July 23, 1967), p. 8.

7. "Kenneth Patchen, Naturalist of the Public Nightmare," *Bird in the Bush*, p. 95.

8. Here Rexroth has translated part of the sixth poem of *The Tao Tê Ching*, by Lao Tzu. For a scholarly English version of the entire book see *The Way of Lao Tzu*, translated by Wing-tsit Chan (Indianapolis and New York, 1963).

9. Quoted by D. T. Suzuki, *Zen Buddhism*, edited by William Barrett (Garden City, New York, 1956), p. 34.

10. No pagination.

11. Lawrence Lipton, "Rexroth," *Los Angeles Free Press,* Part II (January 10, 1969), p. 23. Unfortunately, instead of going into *The Collected Longer Poems* in any detail, Lipton adds some brief generalizations to excerpts from his earlier writings on Rexroth. One statement is false: "In the last decade there has been little or no poetry from his hand. . . ." Apparently he overlooked the sections of new poems in *Natural Numbers* and *The Collected Shorter Poems,* as well as *The Heart's Garden / The Garden's Heart*—an impressive output to be included with the republication of earlier work.

12. Robert Stock, "The Hazards of Art," *The Nation,* CCVIII, 12 (March 24, 1969), 378.

13. Letter #150, in *The Selected Letters of William Carlos Williams,* edited and with an introduction by John C. Thirlwall (New York, 1957), p. 232.

14. Williams, "Verse with a Jolt to It," p. 5.

15. Williams, "Two New Books by Kenneth Rexroth," p. 182.

16. Eberhart, "A Voyage of the Spirit," p. 25.

17. Foster, "The Voice of the Poet," p. 378.

18. "Interview with Kenneth Rexroth," conducted by Cyrena N. Pondrom on March 23, 1968, in Madison, Wisconsin, and published in *Contemporary Literature,* X, 3 (Summer, 1969), 313-31.

19. *Ibid.*

20. *An Autobiographical Novel,* p. 152.

21. *Ibid.*

22. W. B. Yeats, "The Philosophy of Shelley's Poetry," *Essays and Introductions* (London, 1961), p. 65.

23. George Santayana, *Three Philosophical Poets, Lucretius, Dante, and Goethe* (Cambridge, 1944), p. 10.

24. *Ibid.,* p. 11.

25. Susanne Langer, *Feeling and Form* (New York, 1953), p. 219.

26. Denis Saurat, *Literature and the Occult Tradition* (Port Washington, New York, 1966), pp. 56-57.

27. L. S. Dembo, *Conceptions of Reality in Modern American Poetry* (Berkeley and Los Angeles, 1966), p. 1.

28. *Ibid.*

29. *Ibid.,* p. 4.

30. *Ibid.,* p. 5.

31. Roy Harvey Pearce, *Continuity of American Poetry* (Princeton, New Jersey, 1961), p. 5.

32. *Assays,* pp. 151-52.

33. Pearce, p. 134.

34. *Ibid.,* p. 5.

35. Stock, p. 378.

36. "Interview," pp. 323-24.

Selected Bibliography

PRIMARY SOURCES

1. Books by Rexroth (arranged in order of publication)

In What Hour. New York: Macmillan, 1940.

The Phoenix and the Tortoise. New York: New Directions, 1944.

Selected Poems of D. H. Lawrence. Edited with Introduction by Rexroth. New York: New Directions, 1947 (reprinted, New York: Viking Press, Compass Books, 1961).

The New British Poets: An Anthology. Edited with Introduction by Rexroth. New York: New Directions, 1949.

The Art of Worldly Wisdom. Prairie City, Illinois: Decker Press, 1949. Reprinted, Sausalito, California: Golden Goose Press, 1953.

The Signature of All Things. New York: New Directions, 1950.

Beyond the Mountains. New York: New Directions; London: Routledge, 1951. Reprinted, San Francisco: City Lights, n.d.

The Dragon and the Unicorn. Norfolk, Connecticut: New Directions, 1952.

Fourteen Poems by O. V. de L. Milosz. Translation by Rexroth. San Francisco: Peregrine Press, 1952.

A Bestiary for My Daughters Mary and Katherine. San Francisco: Bern Porter, 1955.

One Hundred Poems from the Japanese. Translations. New York: New Directions, 1955 (reprinted, New York: New Directions, 1957; paperback, 1964).

One Hundred French Poems. Translations. Highlands, North Carolina: Jargon, 1955.

Thou Shalt Not Kill: A Memorial for Dylan Thomas. Sunnyvale, California: Horace Schwartz, A Goad Publication, 1955.

In Defense of the Earth. New York: New Directions, 1956 (reprinted, London: Hutchison, 1959).

One Hundred Poems from the Chinese. Translations. New York: New Directions, 1956 (reprinted, New York: New Directions, 1965).

Thirty Spanish Poems of Love and Exile. Translations. San Francisco: City Lights Pocket Bookshop, 1956.

Bird in the Bush: Obvious Essays. New York: New Directions, 1959.

Assays. New York: New Directions, 1961.

Poems from the Greek Anthology. Translations with Introduction. Ann Arbor: The University of Michigan Press, 1962.

The Homestead Called Damascus. World Poets Series, New York: New Directions, 1963.

Natural Numbers: New and Selected Poems. New York: New Directions, 1963.

An Autobiographical Novel. Garden City, New York: Doubleday and Company, 1966.

The Collected Shorter Poems. New York: New Directions, 1966.

The Heart's Garden / The Garden's Heart. Cambridge, Massachusetts: Pym Randall Press, 1967.

Classics Revisited. Chicago: Quadrangle Books, 1968.

The Collected Longer Poems. New York: New Directions, 1968.

Pierre Reverdy Selected Poems. Translations with Introduction by Rexroth. New York: New Directions, 1969.

Love in the Turning Year: One Hundred More Poems from the Chinese. New York: New Directions, 1970.

The Alternative Society: Essays from the Other World. New York: Herder and Herder, 1970.

With Eye and Ear. Essays. New York: Herder and Herder, 1970.

American Poetry in the Twentieth Century. Essays. New York: Herder and Herder, 1971.

Sky Sea Birds Trees Earth House Beasts Flowers. Santa Barbara: Unicorn Press, 1971.

2. Long-playing Records of Rexroth Reading His Poetry

San Francisco Poets. New York: Evergreen Records 1, n.d. With Antoninus, Duncan, Ferlinghetti, McClure, Whalen, Ginsberg, and Broughton.

Poetry Readings in "The Cellar." San Francisco: Fantasy Records 7002 [1957]. With Ferlinghetti and jazz accompaniment.

Kenneth Rexroth at the Black Hawk. San Francisco: Fantasy Records 7008 [1960]. With jazz accompaniment.

"Another Spring," "A Sword in a Cloud of Light," "This Night Only," "An Easy Song," "May Day," *Treasury of 100 Modern American Poets,* IX, New York: Spoken Arts, n.d.

3. Interviews

"Interview with Kenneth Rexroth," *Contemporary Literature,* X, 3 (Summer, 1969), 313-31. "Conducted by Cyrena N. Pondrom on March 23, 1968, in Madison, Wisconsin, where Mr. Rexroth read his poetry to a University audience, and in Milwaukee on March 24. Also incorporated are tape-recorded answers to written questions." An in-depth philosophical exploration.

"Kenneth Rexroth," *The San Francisco Poets,* edited by David Meltzer (including his review of Rexroth in the summer of 1969). New York: Ballantine Books, 1971, pp. 9-55.

SECONDARY SOURCES

1. Checklist

HARTZELL, JAMES, and RICHARD ZUMWINKLE. *Kenneth Rexroth / a Checklist of His Published Writings*, with a Foreword by Lawrence Clark Powell. Los Angeles: Friends of the UCLA Library, University of California, 1967. Indispensable for the study of Rexroth's work; based on the extensive collection of his writings in the University of California at Los Angeles Library.

2. Writings on Rexroth

AARON, DANIEL. *Writers on the Left, Episodes in American Literary Communism.* New York: Harcourt, Brace, and World, 1961, p. 341. Notes Rexroth's activities in the John Reed Clubs.
ALLSOP, K. "Beaten," *Spectator,* CCII (March 13, 1959), 350. Links Rexroth superficially with the Beat Generation.
ANONYMOUS. "Big Day for Bards at Bay," *Life,* XLIII, Part 2 (September 9, 1957), 105-8. On the *Howl* trial and poetry Renaissance, with photographs of Rexroth, Ginsberg, Ferlinghetti, and others.
————. "Cool, Cool Bards," *Time,* LXX (December 2, 1957), 71. On "the man who started the poetry-and-jazz trend."
————. "Daddy-O," *New Yorker,* XXXIV (May 3, 1958), 29-30. Also on Rexroth as leader of poetry and jazz movement.
————. "The Last Bohemian," *Time,* LXXXVII (February 25, 1966), 108. Review of *An Autobiographical Novel* as a "splendid piece of Americana."
BEACH, JOSEPH WARREN. *Obsessive Images.* Minneapolis: University of Minnesota Press, 1960, pp. 91, 241, 257-59, 286, 353-59. Praises Rexroth's philosophical poetry.
BISHOP, JOHN. Untitled review of *One Hundred Poems from the Chinese, Comparative Literature,* X (1958), 61-68. Bishop shows the "highest admiration," with some minor criticisms.
BURDICK, EUGENE. "The Innocent Nihilists Adrift in Squaresville," *The Reporter,* XVIII (April 3, 1958), 30-33. Superficial treatment of Rexroth and the Beats.
CAPOUYA, EMILE. "Sad of Mind but Glad of Heart," *Saturday Review,* XLIX (February 12, 1966), 29-30. Favorable review of *An Autobiographical Novel.*
CHUNG, LING. University of Wisconsin doctoral dissertation on Rexroth and other American translators of Chinese poetry, in progress.
CIARDI, JOHN. "One for Rexroth," *In Fact.* New Brunswick, New Jersey: Rutgers University Press, 1962, p. 54. Portrait in verse by a friend.

DEUTSCH, BABETTE. *Poetry in Our Time*. New York: Columbia University Press, 1956, pp. 24-25, 85, 91-92. Brief praise of Rexroth's "deep truth of feeling."

EBERHART, RICHARD. "A Voyage of the Spirit," *New York Times* Section VII (February 15, 1953), p. 25. Review of *The Dragon and the Unicorn*, with special attention to the style: "hard as prose and lithe as lyric."

EIMERL, SAREL. "Compared with Me," *Reporter*, XXXIV (May 19, 1966), 60, 62. Review of *An Autobiographical Novel* considered as social history.

FERLINGHETTI, LAWRENCE. "Horn on *Howl*," *Evergreen Review*, I, 4 (1957), 145-58. Rexroth's testimony on Ginsberg's poem considered in the tradition of biblical prophecy.

FITTS, DUDLEY. "A Poet Abroad," *New Republic*, CXXVIII (February 9, 1953), 19. Reviewing *The Dragon and the Unicorn*, Fitts calls Rexroth a "Mark Twain who had grown up"—a "comic philosopher" who indicts Western civilization.

————. Untitled Note in *New York Times*, Section VII (July 23, 1967), p. 8. Praising *The Collected Shorter Poems*.

FITZGERALD, WILLIAM. "Twenty Years at Hard Labor," *Poetry*, LVII, 11 (November, 1940), 158-60. Review of *In What Hour*, condemning Rexroth for "inadequate assimilation" of various styles and ideas.

FLINT, R. W. "Poets and Their Subjects," *New Republic*, CXXXVI (February 18, 1957), 19. Favorable review of *In Defense of the Earth*.

FOSTER, RICHARD. "With Great Passion, A Kind of Person," *Hudson Review*, XIII, 1 (Spring, 1960), 149-54. An important review of *Bird in the Bush* by a "standard academic" impressed by Rexroth's "philosophy of humane letters" which links him with Eliot, Richards, Tate, and Blackmur.

————. "Lucubrations of an Outside Insider," *Minnesota Review*, III, 1 (Fall, 1962), 130-33. Review of *Assays*, less enthusiastic than Foster's first.

————. "The Voice of the Poet: Kenneth Rexroth," *Minnesota Review*, II, 3 (Spring, 1962), 377-84. Sensitive appreciation of the lyrical, elegiac, and visionary dimensions of Rexroth's poetry.

GIBSON, MORGAN. "Kenneth Rexroth." *Encyclopaedia of World Literature*. Edited by Wolfgang Bernard Fleischman. New York: F. Ungar Publishing Company, 1957. Brief summary of Rexroth's literary career in Volume 3.

————. "Provincial Anarchy" (column), *Kaleidoscope* (Milwaukee underground newspaper), I, 4 (December 8-21, 1967), 5-12. On Rexroth's anarchism of love.

GREGORY, HORACE and MARYA ZATURENSKA. *A History of American*

Poetry 1900-1940. New York: Harcourt, Brace and Company, 1946. Superficial treatment of Rexroth's poetry as "regional verse."

GRIGSBY, GORDON K. "The Presence of Reality: the Poetry of Kenneth Rexroth." An excellent long essay (so far unpublished) on the "clarity, beauty and truth" of Rexroth's poetry.

HUMPHRIES, ROLFE. "Too Much Abstraction," *New Republic*, CIII (August 12, 1940), 221. Review of *In What Hour*, with praise for clear imagery and condemnation of abstract thought in the poems.

JACOBSON, DAN. "America's 'Angry Young Men'; How Rebellious Are the San Francisco Rebels?" *Commentary*, XXIV (December, 1957), 475-79. Superficial condemnation of Rexroth and the Beats.

KAZIN, ALFRED. "Father Rexroth and the Beats," *Reporter*, XXII (March 3, 1960), 54-56. Rexroth is called an "old-fashioned American sorehead" in this review of *Bird in the Bush*.

KEROUAC, JACK. *The Dharma Bums*. New York: Signet Books, 1958. Convincing portrait of Rexroth as the anarchist poet Reinhold Cacoethes.

KRIEGEL, LEONARD. "Rexroth: Citizen of Bohemia," *Nation*, CCII (June 6, 1966), 688-89. Criticizes Rexroth for idealizing himself in *An Autobiographical Novel*.

LIPTON, LAWRENCE. "Notes Toward an Understanding of Kenneth Rexroth with Special Attention to 'The Homestead Called Damascus,'" *Quarterly Review of Literature*, IX, 2 (1957), 37-46. Indispensable introduction to the complexity of Rexroth's personality and philosophical quest, by a writer who has been his friend since the 1920's.

————. "The Poetry of Kenneth Rexroth," *Poetry*, XC, 3 (June, 1957), 168-80. Most detailed examination of Rexroth's prosody so far.

————. *The Holy Barbarians*. New York: Julian Messmer, Inc., 1959. Considerable reference to Rexroth's ideas in this discussion of the Beats and youth revolt.

————. "Rexroth," *Los Angeles Free Press*, Part II (January 10, 1969), pp. 1 and 22-23. Review of *The Collected Shorter Poems* and *The Collected Longer Poems*, consisting mostly of excerpts from Lipton's earlier writings on Rexroth.

McCARTHY, MARY. *The Groves of Academe*. New York: Harcourt, Brace, 1952. Unflattering portrait of the "poet of the masses."

MILLER, HENRY. "Poems That Grow Like Flowers," *San Francisco Chronicle* (February 10, 1957). Review of Chinese translations.

MILLS, RALPH J. "Recent Prose," *Poetry*, CII, 4 (July, 1963), 270. Brief praise of *Assays*.

MONTAGUE, JOHN. "American Pegasus," *Studies*, XLVIII (Summer, 1959), 183-91. Irish writer's appreciation of Rexroth.

MOOREHOUSE, FRANK. "The American Poet's Visit," *Sidney* (Australia) *Southerly*, XXVIII (1968), 275-85.

PARKINSON, THOMAS. "Phenomenon or Generation." *A Casebook on the Beat*. New York: Thomas Y. Crowell Company, 1961. Useful discussion of Rexroth's leading role in the Bay Area avant-garde, in a collection containing other pertinent writings.

PODHORETZ, NORMAN. "A Howl of Protest in San Francisco," *The New Republic*, CXXXVII (September 16, 1957), 20. Criticizes Rexroth and the Poetry Renaissance for immaturity.

POWELL, LAWRENCE CLARK. "In the Words of Kenneth Rexroth," *New York Times*, Section VII (November 22, 1964), p. 2. Review of Frank Norris' *McTeague*, with praise for Rexroth's Afterword and his poems.

RODMAN, SELDEN. "Gnomic, Fastidious Verses," *New York Herald Tribune* (May 7, 1950), p. 22. Admiration for Rexroth's observation of nature in *The Signature of All Things*.

ROSENTHAL, M. L. "Rexroth: the Fact and the Fury," *Nation*, CLXXXV (September 28, 1957), 199-200. Favorable review of *In Defense of the Earth* as "poems of *fact* in all its irreversibility."

————. "Outside the Academy." *The Modern Poets*. New York: Oxford University Press, 1960. Extension of the review, linking Rexroth with Allen Ginsberg and the "west-coast Renascents."

RUKEYSER, MURIEL. "Lyrical 'Rage,'" *Saturday Review*, XL (November 9, 1957), 15. Review of *In Defense of the Earth* that covers the full range of feeling in the book.

SCOTT, WINFIELD TOWNLEY. "The Dragon and the Unicorn," *New York Herald Tribune*, Vol. XXIX (February 1, 1953), p. 8. Finds Rexroth "always interesting."

SORRENTINO, GIL. "Good House," *Poetry*, CIV (June, 1964), 179-81. Reviewing *Natural Numbers*, he considers Rexroth a "populist" poet in relation to Williams.

STAFFORD, WILLIAM. "A Five Foot Shelf," *Poetry*, CXI (December, 1967), 184-88. Review of *The Collected Shorter Poems* as poetry of truth.

STOCK, ROBERT. "The Hazards of Art," *Nation*, CCVIII, 12 (March 24, 1969), 378. Review of *The Collected Longer Poems*; cites Rexroth as an important influence on the New Left.

UNTERECKER, JOHN. "Calling the Heart to Order," *New York Times*, Section VII (July 23, 1967), p. 8. Favorable review of *The Collected Shorter Poems*.

VAN GHENT, DOROTHE BENDON. Introduction and "Kenneth Rexroth" (Chapter V) in "Some Problems of Communication,"

Master of Arts Thesis (Oakland, California: Mills College, 1935), pp. 1-15 and 94-123. The earliest, and philosophically the most sophisticated discussion so far, of the technique of dissociation in the early Cubist poems of Rexroth, in relation to the works of Gertrude Stein and Laura Riding.

WILLIAMS, WILLIAM CARLOS. "Verse with a Jolt to It," *New York Times*, Section VII (January 28, 1951), p. 5. High praise for the style of *Beyond the Mountains*.

—————. "Letter to Marianne Moore." *The Selected Letters of William Carlos Williams*. Edited by John C. Thirlwall. New York: McDowell, Obilensky, 1957. Criticism of the style of *The Dragon and the Unicorn*.

—————. "Two New Books by Kenneth Rexroth," *Poetry*, XC (June, 1957), 180-90. Careful analysis of the prosody of *In the Defense of the Earth* and *One Hundred Poems from the Chinese*.

Index

151